THE LITTLE GIANT® BOOK OF
BASKETBALL FACTS

THE LITTLE GIANT® BOOK OF
BASKETBALL FACTS

Wayne Stewart

Sterling Publishing Co., Inc.
New York

Library of Congress Cataloging-in-Publication Data

Stewart, Wayne, 1951-
  The Little Giant Book of Basketball Facts/ Wayne Stewart
     p. cm.
  Includes index.
   ISBN 1-4027-2415-2
  1. Basketball—Miscellanea—Juvenile literature. I. Title.
  GV885.13.S74 2005
  796.323'64'0973—dc22

                                              2005001145

10 9 8 7 6 5 4 3 2 1

Published by Sterling Publishing Co., Inc.
387 Park Avenue South, New York, NY 10016
© 2005 by Wayne Stewart
Distributed in Canada by Sterling Publishing
c/o Canadian Manda Group, 165 Dufferin Street
Toronto, Ontario, Canada M6K 3H6
Distributed in Great Britain and Europe by Chris Lloyd at Orca Book
Services, Stanley House, Fleets Lane, Poole BH15 3AJ, England
Distributed in Australia by Capricorn Link (Australia) Pty. Ltd.
P.O. Box 704, Windsor, NSW 2756, Australia

Manufactured in China

Sterling ISBN 1-4027-2415-2

For information about custom editions, special sales, premium and
corporate purchases, please contact Sterling Special Sales
Department at 800-805-5489 or specialsales@sterlingpub.com.

To Great Friends:

Jack Haught, a knowledgeable basketball fan who has provided me with help and ideas over the years.

The Oslowski family—Bill, Marsha, Jean Anne, Joel, and Jeremy—from my hometown of Donora

The Patch family: Rich, who goes all the way back with me to first grade and our days of talking sports on the playground; his wife Paulette; and their children Ben and Kelly.

And, as always, to my wife Nancy and sons Sean and Scott.

CONTENTS

Note to readers: All the statistics in this book were through 2004 unless otherwise stated. The reader should also know that ppg stands for the average points per game a player scored; rpg means rebounds per game; and apg represents the player's assists per game.

1 DID YOU KNOW...?

It's a long time trip from today's basketball scene to the beginnings of the game. Dr. James Naismith invented basketball when he set out to devise an indoor sport that could be played throughout the wicked winters of New England. In 1891, he got the idea of placing a peach basket up high in a YMCA located in Springfield, Massachusetts, and that gave birth to the game of basketball. Since then, many fascinating things have occurred to help shape modern-day basketball.

Test your basketball knowhow with these interesting facts dealing with the rich heritage of basketball as well as present-day play.

One year after Dr. Naismith introduced the game of roundball, a physical education teacher named Senda Berenson modified the game for play by women, doing so at Smith College in Massachusetts. Her rules included players being forbidden to steal the ball or dribble more than three times. In addition, the court was split into three sections, with each player confined to play in a given area.

The rules eventually evolved, and by the 1960s the women's game began to more closely resemble what is seen nowadays.

The first college to organize a team was Geneva College in Beaver Falls, Pennsylvania. That's the same hometown of quarterback Joe Namath. Shortly, several other colleges jumped on board, including Iowa in 1893, Ohio State and Temple in 1894, and Yale the following year.

The NBA's roots date to 1946. The average salary for a pro player back then was a paltry $4,500 per season. Of course, back then the average height was also on the tiny side—at around 6' 4" tall.

College basketball's first NCAA first tournament dates back to 1939 and included a field of just eight teams, with Oregon winning it all. It was hardly an earth-shattering event then, but the yearly tournament, with its climactic Final Four, has now become a global event.

The National Invitation Tournament (NIT) began one year earlier and for many years was considered more prestigious than the NCAA event.

One year the same team won both of basketball's biggest tournaments—the NIT and the NCAA. In 1949–1950, City College of New York managed this feat and by beating the same team, Bradley, in the finals of both tournaments.

•

Byron "Whizzer" White was a college basketball star who, in 1937–1938, led his Colorado squad to its first championship when it shared the Big Seven Conference title with Utah. White was also an All-American football player in college, and went on to become a United States Supreme Court justice.

When the upstart Detroit Pistons knocked off the much more glamorous Los Angeles Lakers in 2004, the contrast between the two teams was enormous. The Lakers' roster featured players who had appeared in a grand total of 40 All-Star games, while the Pistons had a mere four appearances spread among a few of its players.

When it came to matchups, the Pistons looked out of their league. For example, while the Lakers' center was the famous Shaquille O'Neal (7' 1" and 350 pounds), the Pistons had to counter with Ben Wallace, a man who gave away four inches and a whopping 110 pounds to O'Neal.

According to one survey of NBA experts, the strongest players ever to suit up were Wilt Chamberlain at 7' 1" and 275 pounds, followed by fellow centers Willis Reed, the ursine Wes Unseld, and the towering Artis Gilmore, the only other seven-footer on the list.

Coach Hubie Brown said of Gilmore, ". . . you could hit him with an axe and he'd still take you to the rim. He was as strong as anybody." Had this list been compiled later, it would seem Shaquille O'Neal and, no doubt, a few other more recent players, would have been added.

Terry Pluto wrote about the time that Chamberlain was coaching in the ABA when a fight broke out. He left his seat on the bench, went onto the court, and hoisted Mel Daniels, one of the strongest men in the league, up "as if he were a toothpick." When the teammates of Daniels saw this turn of events, they decided to leave the court, returning peacefully to their bench.

Through the end of the 20th century, Boston Celtics players had carried off 10 total Most Valuable Player awards. In all, four different men accomplished this: Larry Bird, Dave Cowens, Bob Cousy, and Bill Russell. Strangely, that longstanding franchise had never produced a player to lead the league in scoring.

•

When the Denver Nuggets and the Detroit Pistons squared off on December 13, 1983, the final tally resulted in the highest scoring game in NBA history.

At the end of regulation play, the teams were locked at 145 apiece. Many shots later, the Pistons pulled out a 186–184 victory in triple overtime. In all, six scoring records were shattered, with Kiki Vandeweghe leading all scorers with 51 markers.

For a lengthy streak back in the 1971–1972 season, the Los Angeles Lakers simply could not lose. The old record for consecutive wins had been 20, but the Lakers annihilated that standard, winning 33 in a row! When they won their 33rd, it had been an incredible 68 days since they had last lost a contest.

On January 9, 1972, the winning finally ended as L.A. lost to the team which had held the former winning streak record, the Milwaukee Bucks. Still, the Lakers went on to rack up a 69–13 season, then the record for the most wins ever for a season. The Lakers also won the NBA title that season in a five-game set versus the Knicks.

Standouts on this remarkable team included a 35-year-old Wilt Chamberlain, Jerry West at the age of 33, Gail Goodrich, and Happy Hairston.

In 1951, a strange game took place which left fans
(the ones who had stuck it out) fatigued and players
totally exhausted. This game, between the Rochester
Royals and the Indianapolis Olympians, was, in fact,
the longest game in pro basketball history. It lasted six
overtime sessions before Rochester finally pulled it out,
75–73.

Since the game was played before the inception of
the 24-second clock, the players weren't quite as tired as
one might expect—from time to time both teams sat on
the ball in O.T. For example, neither team managed a
single point in either the second or fourth overtime
period and the point total for their entire overtime play
was a measly 18.

It was during a double overtime loss by the Chicago Bulls at the hands of the Celtics in the first round of the 1985–1986 playoffs that Michael Jordan drained the ball through the hoop, which gave him 63 points. That set a record for the most points ever in an NBA playoff game.

What made it even more awe inspiring were the facts that Jordan was only in his second season in the league and he wasn't even supposed to be on the court that day. Doctors had told him after he had broken his foot just three games into the season that he shouldn't play again until the following year. Instead, he came back on March 15th, more than a month before his 63-point outburst. He even played in 53 of the game's 58 minutes.

Julius Erving was a star forward long before his days in the NBA. Erving toiled in a league known as the American Basketball Association (ABA) which tried to compete with the NBA many years ago. Ultimately the ABA didn't last, but it gave birth to many greats, including the man known as Dr. J.

During the final three years of play before the ABA died out, Erving, who averaged 28.7 points per game (ppg) over his ABA career, led his New Jersey Nets, who went on to join the NBA, to championships twice. Later he went on to play for the Philadelphia 76'ers, where he enjoyed even more success and fame.

If you combine all the points Dr. J scored in both leagues, it adds up to 30,026. Few men have ever reached the 30,000-point plateau, but Dr. J did with relative ease and grace, swooping high in the sky for many a dramatic dunk and acrobatic shot.

George Mikan was voted the greatest basketball player in the first half of the 20th century. The NBA's first superstar stood high above the rest of the players both literally (at 6' 10") and figuratively. Even his jersey number was higher—he wore #99.

Mikan's main weapon was a lethal hook shot, which helped him corral six straight scoring titles. He guided the old Minneapolis Lakers to six titles over a seven-year period. A teammate of his once summed it up by saying, "In our time, George was Michael Jordan, Magic Johnson, and Larry Bird all rolled into one." And Bob Cousy chipped in with, "He was unmovable. He was so much stronger than anyone in the league at that time."

One of the flashiest players of all-time was Pete Maravich. His no-look passes stunned observers and his dribbling skills were second to none. Throughout the 1970s, only three men scored more points in the NBA than the sensation from Louisiana State University.

Maravich was such a great scorer that, when he poured in 68 points on February 25th of 1977, only two men, Chamberlain and Elgin Baylor, had ever recorded a higher output in a single contest. His scoring surge represented the most points ever scored by a guard in NBA annals.

During the 1976–1977 seasons, "Pistol Pete" became just the fourth guard in NBA history to average over 30 ppg. It's no wonder that in 1996 he was selected to the NBA's Top 50 Players list.

Maravich's scoring prowess began in college. During each of his collegiate seasons at LSU, Maravich averaged between 43 and 45 ppg. He led the NCAA in scoring three years in a row and, naturally, was an All-American those seasons.

Norm Van Lier set a few records for assists during his roundball career. He was a fine player, mainly with the Chicago Bulls. In 1970–1971, he led the NBA in assists, averaging 10.1 per game (then as a member of the Cincinnati Royals).

Then along came Kevin Porter with his amazing assist feats, which surpassed Van Lier. Porter led the league in playmaking four times, twice with Washington, one year as a Detroit Piston, and one year in which he split time with Detroit and New Jersey.

In 1978, Porter became the first man ever to register 1,000 or more assists in a season when he racked up 1,099 to shatter the old record of 910. He even set the all-time single game high with 29 assists, a record since broken.

The strange thing about the records of Porter and Van Lier is the fact that both men went to the same rather obscure college, St. Francis (in Pennsylvania). Porter starred there into the early 1970s, while Van Lier played there earlier, in the late 1960s.

Wilt Chamberlain held the record for the most assists in a game by a player who was not a guard. Hard to believe, but the gigantic Chamberlain recorded 21 assists during a contest in 1968.

One could call Chuck Cooper the Jackie Robinson of the NBA in that he was the first African American to enter the NBA, doing so three years after Robinson's entry into major league baseball in 1947.

Cooper, out of Duquesne, signed with the Boston Celtics and was followed a few weeks later by Sweetwater Clifton. Clifton had appeared with the Harlem Globetrotters, was spotted by the New York Knicks, and was signed by them to an NBA contract.

The same year Chuck Cooper was drafted, Earl Lloyd was too. When Lloyd's Washington Capitals' schedule had them playing before Cooper's Celtics, Lloyd actually became the first African-American to *appear* in an NBA contest. That historic game took place on October 31, 1950. Further, Lloyd became the first African-American to win an NBA championship in 1955 when he was with Syracuse.

Scottie Pippen was a member of six NBA championships. He was slightly overshadowed by Michael Jordan, but that's hardly unusual. Pippen was adept both on defense, usually guarding the other team's best player, and on offense, using his quickness and speed.

Pippen received what may be his greatest compliment when he was named as one of the 50 Greatest Players in NBA History.

Rony Seikaly had a highly unusual youth. His father was an overseas businessman, so Rony was born and spent his early years in the volatile city of Beirut, Lebanon before moving to Athens, Greece.

Once some terrorists exploded a stairway in the Beirut apartment building where Rony's family lived. His life was spared because he was, at the exact moment of the explosion, on the elevator, having decided not to use the stairs that fateful day. After an incident such as that, life in the trenches of the NBA paint seemed almost tame for the 6' 11" center.

Growing up on foreign soil back then actually hurt Seikaly's playing skills. He played in Greece against inferior talent and with little or no strong coaching. Then, after participating in a basketball camp under Syracuse coach Jim Boeheim, Seikaly decided he wanted to spend his college days under Boeheim's guidance. His statistics climbed each year from only 8.1 ppg as a freshman to 16.3 by his senior year.

Rony enjoyed an NBA career playing for the Miami Heat, the Golden State Warriors, the Orlando Magic, and the New Jersey Nets.

From the Foul Line

When Mark Price retired, he had sunk just over 90% of his foul shots (.904) to rank number one all-time.

The man who ranked just behind Price clicked on exactly 90% of his NBA free throws. That man, Rick Barry, succeeded using a most unusual style, one usually reserved for little kids not yet strong enough to shoot the ball all the way up to the 10-feet tall rim—Barry shot underhand, also known as "granny style."

Barry gave logical reasons as to why his underhand method of shooting foul shots made sense and why it worked so well for him. He felt it was "easier to shoot my way . . . especially in the late stages of a game, when you're tired, and not able to do all the things as easily as you have been earlier in the game. Your arms may be hanging down at your sides because you're tired.

"So isn't it sensible that on free throws you would want to conserve your strength as much as possible and shoot them underhanded? Your arms already are in position to shoot—hanging at your sides—and you don't have to bring them overhead."

Rick's sons Brent and Jon shoot well but didn't use their father's methods. Through the 2003–2004 season, Brent was a .820 career shooter from the line, while Jon connected on .847 of his free throw shots. A third son, Drew, shot a respectable, but hardly noteworthy, .774 at the charity stripe in just 31 career attempts.

●

For single-season free-throw accuracy, Calvin Murphy reigns as the best ever, connecting at a .958 clip. The 5' 9" Murphy had a shot so sweet one columnist called it as "soft as cotton puffs in a wastebasket."

Murphy is the answer to a strange trivia item as he's the only NBA star ever to claim a national championship in baton twirling, which he did as a teenager in 1963. They say he picked up a twirler's baton even before he did a basketball. He inherited both interests from his mother, Ina, a one-time majorette and a semi-pro basketball guard.

When it comes to sizzling foul shooting over a torrid stretch, the record belongs to Michael Williams of the Minnesota Timberwolves. From March 24, 1993, until November 9th of the next season, he never missed a free throw, stringing together 97 on-the-money shots in a row.

Rich Kelley was the center for the Jazz in 1978–1979, and he established a rather offbeat record for a player 7' or taller. He clicked for an impressive .814 free throw percentage, topping former record holder Don Otten of the Fort Wayne Pistons (.799).

Those totals are light years ahead of men such as Wilt Chamberlain. By way of contrast, the best year Chamberlain ever had at the charity stripe was a pathetic .613, and that was almost exactly 100 percentage points higher than what he shot on average over his entire 14-year career.

Like Chamberlain, Shaquille O'Neal suffered at the free throw line. During his fourth and fifth NBA seasons. he shot a miserable .487 and .484 from the line.

Through the 2003–2004 season, he had played 158 all-important playoff games, sinking just over half of his foul shots at .518. After awhile, opposing players felt that in certain circumstances it was better to foul O'Neal than allow him easy dunks. After all, a dunk was a sure thing, whereas with O'Neal at the line there was a good chance he'd miss at least one attempted shot. The media dubbed this ploy "Hack-a-Shaq."

Jamal Mashburn is so well rounded he was one of only three players in the NBA to rank in the top 30 in scoring, rebounding, and assists in 2000–01.

He shared the Dallas Mavericks record with a career-high 50 points scored in a single game on Nov. 12, 1994, and was the second youngest player in the league's history to score at least 50 in a game (Rick Barry was 87 days younger).

Derek Harper was one NBA player who got better every year. Incredibly, from his rookie season until his ninth season in the NBA, his scoring average rose. The numbers: 5.7 ppg in 1983–1984; 9.6; 12.2; 16.0; 17.0; 17.3; 18.0; and 19.7 in 1990–1991. Perhaps it wasn't that tough to improve during, say, his first four seasons, but once his average hit 16 or so, he amazed fans by continuing his trend.

The ABA lasted nine seasons and only two players were in that league from day one up to the day it collapsed. The men were center Byron Beck of Denver Rockets and Louie Dampier of the Kentucky Colonels.

While Beck was solid (12.0 ppg), little Louie, a 6' guard, finished as the lifetime leader in several categories, including total points (13,726), assists (4,004), and minutes played.

Dampier was also the league's best three-point artists, connecting on 794 long-range shots and did so at a .358 percentage.

In 1998, a new feature was added to the events of the NBA All-Star Weekend, namely All-Star 2ball. That contest matched players from the NBA and the WNBA from the same cities in a timed shooting contest.

When Jeff Hornacek of the Utah Jazz teamed up with Natalie Williams of the Utah Starzz and won the 2ball title, he became the first player to win that *and* the three-point shootout in the same year.

While the ABA did endure for nearly one decade, there was little stability in that league. Teams shifted cities and franchises folded like a cheap lawn chair. In its final season, the ABA was down from two divisions to only one.

Only three of the franchises finished in the same city in which they had begun: Indiana, winner of three ABA titles; Kentucky, which won a championship; and Denver.

A great quote on the old league's woes came from Mike Green, who spent time in both the ABA and the NBA. When asked what he felt was the biggest differences between the leagues, he replied, "In the NBA you get paid."

By 2002–2003, German-born Dirk Nowitzki was the sixth most prolific scorer in league, averaging 25.1 ppg for the Dallas Mavericks. One of his rewards for such play was his third berth for an NBA All-Star game.

One of Nowitzki's first chances to showcase his talent came when he played on the 1996 German National Junior Team, German Under-22 National Team, European Junior Select Team, and the World Junior Select Team. In 1998, he became an NBA first round pick. In 2000, he was selected to participate in the Schick Rookie Challenge during the All-Star Weekend.

Nowitzki's boyhood idol, Scottie Pippen, evaluated him: "He's probably the only power forward that I've seen that can do the things that he can do out on the court, being a seven-footer." After all, how many big men can sink three-pointers and also drive to the hoop with ease?

Hal Greer was a fantastic guard for 15 seasons, beginning in 1958. Back then such a long career was highly unusual, but Greer, a Marshall University great, took care of himself. Lightning quick, he was still pumping in around 22 ppg until his last few seasons en route to entering the exclusive 20,000 point circle. He was one of the main reasons his Philadelphia 76'ers won the 1967 NBA crown.

Greer had a unique approach to his foul shooting—he'd get up to the line, grab the ball, then take each and every free throw as a jump shot. He explained that when he was shooting jumpers from the field he was, in a way, practicing his foul shooting and, when he was at the line, he was practicing his outside jump shooting at the same time.

Isiah Lord Thomas was one of the greatest guards ever. In 1981, after his sophomore season with the Indiana Hoosiers, in which they won the NCAA championship season, he entered the NBA Draft. He was the second pick in the draft, selected by the Detroit Pistons. From his rookie season with the Pistons until his retirement in 1994, Isiah excelled.

Thomas possessed blazing speed. He was the driving force behind his Detroit Pistons back-to-back titles in 1989 and 1990, the year he won the MVP in the NBA Finals.

Thomas was selected to 12 All-Star teams and won that event's MVP twice. He was elected into the Hall of Fame in 2000 after displaying so many hoop skills over so many years.

Thomas could handle and pass the ball with the best of them, and he fell just shy of the 20,000-point plateau. When he quit, the 6' 1" dynamic leader was one of only four men to amass 9,000+ assists, and his exact point total stood at 18, 822, the all-time record for a player wearing the Pistons uniform.

As a junior in high school, Isiah Thomas already stood out from the crowd. One coach said of the future Hall of Famer, "He's strong, quick, fast, an excellent jumper with great timing. Has great hands and tremendous reactions. . . he wins."

•

When Wilt Chamberlain joined the NBA, only four men stood taller than 6' 9". In Mark Heisler's book *Giants: The 25 Greatest Centers of All Time*, he wrote of the time Elgin Baylor addressed the topic of Chamberlain's superhuman strength. Baylor recalled the time when "Wilt went up to dunk the ball and Dick Barnett [a Knicks guard] jumped on him and grabbed him by the neck. And he took him from the floor, up in the air— you ask Barnett about it—and dunked the ball." Baylor added that Chamberlain even did that against several big centers who tried to hold him by his shoulders. "He just went up and dunked the ball."

Players openly admit that they can be hurt by aspects of the game that they have no control over. For instance, players can hear the boos and taunts that sometimes cascade down on them from the stands. Also, they often hate to be traded, uprooted from their homes, and shipped to a new city.

When Adrian Dantley was 23 he was swapped to Utah, his third time traded. Entering his fourth pro season, he was playing for his fourth team. In an issue of *Basketball Digest*, Dantley spoke of how he "had tears coming out of my eyes, and I haven't had tears coming out of my eyes in a long time." He continued, "I'm glad I'm not married. I would hate to put a family through this."

Kareem Abdul-Jabbar listed other intangibles that can get to a player. First of all, he felt the season was too long and grueling. He believed fans lost interest in regular season games as the year wound on and on and on. Some players even suggest that they can't play at their peak due to the demanding 82-game schedule.

Abdul-Jabbar also griped about the extensive travel players must endure. In a *Basketball Digest* issue, he said, "The way we play now, it's totally impossible to play nearly all out all the time, and that's another problem. It takes experience to learn when to pick your spots for all-out effort."

When Yao Ming was selected by the Rockets as the first overall pick in the 2002 draft, he had already averaged 23.5 ppg and 15.4 rebounds per game (rpg) for five seasons while playing for the Shanghai Sharks (in the China Basketball Association). Even with so many fine seasons behind him, Ming was only 22 years old when the Rockets drafted him.

A great name from the "old days" of the NBA was 6' 8"
Dolph Schayes. An All-Star twelve times over his 15-year
career, this man, who played both forward and center for
the Syracuse Nationals and the Philadelphia 76'ers, was
one of the early stars of the game.

Schayes played in the first All-Star game ever back
on March 2, 1951, using his patented set shot.

Robert Parish, known as the "Chief," wore a rather strange number on his jersey, #00. It's been said that he got that number because when he was in high school and they were passing out uniforms, they ran out of ones with numbers on them.

Parish went on to play at Centenary college, which had had only 750 students enrolled. Still, if a player has talent, scouts will discover him, and Golden State drafted him.

Parish was involved in what some people have called the most lopsided NBA trade ever. After spending four seasons with the Warriors, he was beginning to show real promise. He was peddled to the Boston Celtics with a first-round pick (which the Celtics used to acquire Kevin McHale) in exchange for two first-round selections. Both Parish and McHale rolled on, winning a slew of games for Boston.

Hakeem Olajuwon came to the United States from Nigeria when he was 17 years old. Remarkably, the man who would become an NBA superstar had not played basketball until he was 16.

In just a few short years he was a star at the University of Houston, and later made a stellar living mainly with the Houston Rockets.

By the time Tim Duncan was 27 years old he had won two NBA championships, including a gratifying win that ended the Chicago Bulls "three-peat" reign in 1998–1999, and two MVP trophies over his six seasons as a pro.

From 1998 through 2003, no man recorded as many double-doubles as Duncan did.

The Los Angeles Lakers won five NBA titles during their glorious decade of the 1980s. Only three men were there for each championship: Kareem Abdul-Jabbar, Magic Johnson, and Michael Cooper.

During his days at UCLA Abdul-Jabbar was known as Lew Alcindor. Back then, one team in his conference went to great lengths to prepare their players for the daunting task of trying to shoot over Alcindor's towering frame. During practice, a player would act out the part of Alcindor and plays would be run against him. To better authenticate how difficult it would be to face him, the player was given a tennis racket to swat away any shot he could then reach.

Another UCLA grad who changed his name was Walt Hazzard, later known as Mahdi Abdul-Rahman. He was a 6' 3" All-American guard who began playing basketball on the playgrounds of Philadelphia and attended Overbrook High School, one of the most famous high schools in the United States when it comes to producing basketball players.

Hazzard spoke of running the fast break in *On Court with the Superstars of the NBA*. He said that to execute the break well is "probably the most important thing a playmaker does. The idea is to get a three-on-two or two-on-one or four-on-three situation, get an easy shot before the defense can get back into position." In other words, he said, "once you've gotten the overload situation, your team makes sure to exploit it."

Once Bill Walton was asked which player played the toughest defense against him during his college career. Now, although he had certainly faced some stiff competition, his reply came as a surprise. He said that during team workouts at UCLA one of his own teammates, Swen Nater, was his most challenging foe.

The 6' 11" Nater was Walton's backup center for the Bruins and later spent 11 seasons in the pros. Nater, who averaged only about three minutes of play per game over his two-year reserve role backing up Walton in college, once commented in a *Basketball Digest* article, "I'll always play in Bill's shadow. I'm always compared to Bill. I always hear, 'Bill's so great,' and I don't mind. It's true." He added, "I'm always asked about Bill, but, funny, Bill is never asked about me."

When Nater's unsung playing days as a Bruin were through, he was drafted by both the Virginia Squires of the ABA and the Milwaukee Bucks of the NBA. He decided to go with Virginia because he realized if he signed with the Bucks, he'd again be playing the role of backup center to yet another UCLA great, Kareem Abdul-Jabbar.

•

Larry Bird was one of the best players ever at shooting with his off hand. Normally he'd shoot the ball right-handed, but when it was to his advantage to shoot lefty, he was quite adept—and not just at lay-ups or very short jumpers.

If Bird wasn't, by definition, ambidextrous, he was pretty darn close to it. It's a fact that Bird uses his left hand to write, but mainly made his living with his sweet right-handed, shoot-from-anywhere jumper.

While NBA players get out in the open court to run and gun quite a bit, they also have definite, set plays at their disposal. Jo Jo White, a marvelous guard, once said that teams he played on, such as the Celtics, went to their plays only when they weren't pushing the ball up court, running plays especially when they wanted to take advantage of certain situations. For instance, if the opponents' center was in foul trouble, they'd want to get the ball in the hands of their own center. The Celtics would have several options in such circumstances.

White said the plays weren't all that complicated, but they provided every player with a plan of where to be and what to do while on the attack. He stated, "We're not fooling the other team—they probably know our plays as well as we do, just as we know their plays after facing them a few times in the season." The keys are simple: how well will the defense adjust to the plays called and how well will the team on offense execute its plays?

Perhaps the most famous and amazing shot ever made in WNBA history came when Teresa Weatherspoon heaved a desperation shot from past the mid-court stripe as seconds ticked away at the end of Game #2 of the 1999 Championship. The shot went in, to give the Liberty a 68–67 victory over the Houston Comets.

Weatherspoon spent her childhood in Pineland, Texas, which had a population of only 882. She wears uniform #11 in memory of her favorite uncle, who passed away when she was 11 years old.

Amos Alonzo Stagg is considered one of the greatest football coaches of all-time. As head coach for the University of Chicago for 41 seasons, the College of the Pacific for 14 more years, and later, punting coach at Stockton Junior College in California, he is credited with changing the face of football. It was he who first sent a man in motion, had his teams make backfield shifts, and came up with the quick kick, the end around, and even the lateral. The NCAA Division III playoff championship game is named in Stagg's honor. It's not surprising, then, to learn he was inducted into football's Hall of Fame.

Few people know, though, that Stagg helped Dr. James Naismith in the early development of basketball. Stagg introduced the game of basketball at the University of Chicago, was also a highly successful roundball coach, and is a member of the basketball Hall of Fame.

Just before the 2004–2005 NCAA season began, Wake Forest coach Skip Prosser knew his talented sophomore guard Chris Paul was going to make a huge impact on his program. He told the Associated Press that he wanted Paul to go out on the court and play instinctively, without thinking. Prosser explained, "One of the hardest things for Chris to understand last year was that I trust him completely. I want him to play, not to think."

Paul, at an even six-feet (or an inch less, depending upon what source is used), wound up getting more votes than any other NCAA 2004–2005 player in the preseason All-America team. Previously, Tim Duncan was the only Wake player to earn that honor.

By the end of his second season as a Demon Deacon, Paul averaged 6.6 apg and, according to some experts, was "the best point guard, and perhaps player, in the nation." He was called "a lethal scorer and playmaker, with outstanding quickness and penetration abilities." One web site said Paul might be the best point guard to enter the NBA draft since Jason Kidd left college for the pro ranks in 1994.

2 QUICK QUIZZES

Test your basketball IQ with these interesting facts and anecdotes. The answers are on pages 58 to 63.

1. Name the point guard known for his long hair and longer jump shots. The former Santa Clara player has developed an uncanny court sense in the NBA and is a master of the pick-and-roll. Although he didn't pan out too well for the Phoenix Suns (who drafted him in 1996) in his first stay there, he did well after going to Dallas.

2. Where was the first National Invitational Tournament (NIT) held?

3. What graduate of Wake Forest won the Rookie of the Year Award for his spectacular play in 1997–1998?

4. What player was Seattle's first-round selection in 1990 and went on to specialize in both offense and defense? He was given the nickname "The Glove" as a tribute to his defense, and became an almost automatic selection on the All-Defensive First Team.

This player was an All-Star guard and was considered to be the Supersonics' best player for 12 straight seasons before he moved on to the Lakers. He is also an iron man, missing just seven games over his first 13 years in the league. Final clue: Although he is not noted for being a great shooter, he still gets the job done, managing to score a ton of points, nevertheless. Name this man.

5. What player took home the first-ever MVP Award? Clue: That honor, also known as the Maurice Podoloff Trophy, was first given out in 1956 and went to a high scorer with the initials B.P.

6. Within five years, when did the San Antonio Spurs begin their first season of play?

7. Name the man who is said to be a small forward who has the ability to do many things well—from his defensive prowess to his jump shot to his competitive nature. His initials are R.J. and he broke into the league in 2001–2002 with the New Jersey Nets.

8. Who holds the record for the most minutes played per game over his career?

9. Who holds the record for the highest average of minutes played per game over one season?

10. Who was the woman who scored the very first basket in WNBA history? Clues: She sank the shot for the Los Angeles Sparks against the New York Liberty on June 21, 1997. Her initials are P.T.

11. Andre Miller is a very dependable point guard who typically scores around 14 or so points each time out. He's also good for about eight assists per game (apg), although in his best season (through 2003–2004) he averaged nearly 11 per contest. Name either his college or the team he spent his rookie year with.

12. Name the two brothers whose last name starts with "M" who both were enshrined in basketball's Hall of Fame.

13. What strong rebounder was called the best defensive center in the NBA in 2003–2004 when his team won the championship?

14. Which NBA team has been the most successful franchise in the history of the game? Clue: It's not a team such as the Chicago Bulls, who enjoyed splendid success lately with the legendary Michael Jordan. Nor is it the glitzy Los Angeles Lakers. Instead, it's a team that had several dynasties a bit deeper back in time.

15. Baron Davis was, by 2003–2004, considered to be one of the best, if not the best, pure point guards in the NBA. He is the type of guard who can both dish the ball and put it in the hoop. What college did he attend?

16. Name the two players who won all five of the Defensive Player of the Year trophies from 1996 through 2001. Clue: they both attended Georgetown University.

17. Who was the next man to win the Defensive Player of the Year award in back-to-back seasons?

18. Name the player who was the first overall draft pick of the WNBA 1999 draft. She was selected out of Tennessee by the Washington Mystics.

19. Name this player. He was a college sensation at Cincinnati and was selected by the New Jersey Nets in the first round (first pick overall) of the 2000 NBA Draft. He was traded to the Denver Nuggets for three future first-round draft choices on July 15, 2004.

This player's career high for points scored in a game is 35 versus Seattle in February of 2003. Twice he's hauled in 21 rebounds from his forward spot on the floor. Additionally, even though he is a big man at 6' 9" he once dished out 11 assists.

20. Name either of the two players who shared Rookie of the Year honors in 1994–1995.

21. After battling through a hospital-load of injuries, this player enjoyed a good season in 2003–2004. He loves to fire his 15–18 foot, face-up shot even though he plays the pivot position. He attended the University of Massachusetts. Name him.

22. Chauncey Billups led all NBA rookies in 1997–1998 in three-pointers made (107) and was third in three-point percentage. By 2003–2004, he had established himself as one of the top two or three point guards in the league. What team did he break in with?

23. How many kids were drafted straight out of high school in 2004 draft?

24. Can you name any one of the first five players picked in the '98 draft? Clue: they had these initials: M.O., M.B., R.L., A.J., and V.C.

25. What small forward spent his rookie season, 1999–2000, and the next three years with the Los Angeles Clippers before moving on to Miami and then to the Lakers? He has playmaking skills to go with his abilities to shoot and to drive to the hole.

26. Name the player who was a member of Team USA for the 2000 Olympics. In 2003, he was swapped from the Milwaukee Bucks to the Seattle SuperSonics in a five-player deal after he had become the Bucks all-time leader in three-pointers made (1,051) and attempted.

This player broke into the league in 1996–97 and was named to the NBA All-Rookie Second Team. He is deadly from the free throw line, at one point ranking eighth in NBA history in free-throw percentage (.882). Who is he?

27. Since 1976–1977 (and through 2003–2004), only three men have finished a season in the top 10 in scoring, assists, and steals. Name one of these players.

28. Who was the first player in the history of the WNBA to reach the 2,000 points plateau?

29. This member of the top 50 players in NBA history dates back to the 1950s and '60s. As a vital part of the Celtics reign, he was also known for his uncanny ability to hit bank shots. During his team's record eight straight titles, he was a heavy scorer and either led or finished second on the team in points from 1963 to 1966.

Only fellow Celtic Bill Russell, with 11, had more championship rings than this player's nine. Who is this name from the past?

30. Within five years, when did the NCAA hold its first national championship for women?

31. In 2003–2004, what player became just the fifth player ever (and the first one in 29 years) to lead the league in total points and total rebounds?

32. Name the guard who was drafted by the Lakers in 1993 out of the University of Cincinnati and who finished in the NBA's top 15 players for assists in eight of his first 11 seasons. He also finished in the top 25 in assist-to-turnover ratio eight years in a row through 2003–2004.

Due to his electrifyingly quick first step, he was given the nickname "Nick the Quick." Then, due to his knack for hitting key shots, he also became known as "Nick at Night." His last name, though not pronounced like the verb, is an apt description of this player.

33. What college program has what is arguably the greatest dynasty in women's college basketball history?

34. Who had an unusual college career in that he was named to ACC All-Rookie team and was on the All-ACC Tournament's second team in his only season of college basketball? As a Duke Blue Devil, he was one of only six players under Coach Mike Krzyzewski to average in double figures as a freshman.

He then went pro with the Magic for his rookie season and then on to Clippers in his second season.

35. Here's a quiz on nicknames of players who were active as the 21st century was ushered in. 1. Who went by "Big Dog"? 2. Give the nickname of Ron Artest. 3. What is Brent Barry sometimes called? 4. What is Andrew DeClerq's nickname? 5. Who is also known as "Air Canada"? 6. Who goes by "Mad Dog"?

36. Although his first name begins with the final letter of the alphabet, he ranks among the best in the business. In 2003–2004, experts said this man was one of the top ten power forwards in the league. Although not a big man for his position (at 6' 9"), he is a high-octane scorer (20.1 ppg in 2003–2004 for Portland). Name this player.

37. What player, labeled a "pogo stick" by one magazine in 2004 for his quick jumping skills, has the initials S.M.? **Clues:** He plays the small forward position, he broke in with Phoenix, and he attended college at the University of Las Vegas at Nevada.

38. Three-time All-Star Paul Pierce is a big guard, who at 6' 6" can play forward as well. When he nailed 2,071 points in 2000–2001, he became the first Celtic to clear the 2000-point mark since another player did that in 1988. Who was that player?

39. Isiah Thomas has always had a fondness for point guards. When he was President of Basketball Operations for the New York Knicks, he saw how effective men such as Damon Stoudamire and Jamaal Tinsley can be.

Who was Thomas speaking of when he said, "A point guard is your quarterback. He has to be a leader with a winning mentality and have the ability to make all those around him better players. He has to lead your team in good times and bad. [He] has all those qualities."

Clues: The player is a native New Yorker whose career was unusual in that his scoring average increased in each of his first five NBA seasons and his shooting percentage also was boosted over his first six seasons.

40. Who was the only Connecticut player ever to score at least 700 points twice in his career and 500 points in his first three seasons? In fact, he averaged a team-high 21.5 ppg and was named Most Outstanding Player of the 1999 NCAA Final Four after scoring 27 points in the Huskies' 77–74 championship game win over Duke.

Answers

1. Steve Nash

2. At Madison Square Garden in New York City

3. Tim Duncan

4. Gary Payton

5. Bob Pettit

6. Originally this franchise opened for business in 1967–1968 as the old Dallas Chaparrals of the ABA, so technically that's the correct answer. Take credit if you said 1973–1974, though, since that's when they first played under the name of the San Antonio Spurs.

7. Richard Jefferson

8. Wilt Chamberlain. He was such an iron man, he racked up an out-of-this world average of 45.8 minutes per game lifetime.

9. Wilt Chamberlain. During the 1961–1962 season, he played in 80 of his team's 82 games and registered an average of 48.5 minutes played per contest.

Since a regulation game lasts 48 minutes, Chamberlain's 48.5 minutes played average means he seemingly played in more minutes per game than is mathematically possible. However, due to his putting in some court time in overtime games and his playing tirelessly in the regulation contests, he was able to rack up all of those minutes.

10. Penny Toler

11. Andre Miller attended Utah and was originally drafted by the Cleveland Cavaliers in the first round of the 1999 Draft.

12. Al McGuire was inducted into the hall in 1992. The following year, his brother Dick also was admitted into that elite organization.

13. Ben Wallace, of the Detroit Pistons

14. The Boston Celtics. Through 2003–2004, they had appeared in 19 NBA Finals and took top honors in a staggering 16 of those seasons to become the New York Yankees of the NBA. It's as if once they made it to the Finals, they became a lock to win it all.

From 1957–1969, the Boston Celtics won 11 championships over 13 years, a feat unmatched in all of professional sports.

15. UCLA

16. Dikembe Mutombo won it for the Atlanta Hawks in 1996–1997 and 1997–1998; and Alonzo Mourning of the Miami Heat, won it the next two seasons. Mutombo came back to win this award again in 2000–2001.

17. In both the 2001–2002 and the 2002–2003 seasons, Ben Wallace of Detroit won it.

18. Chamique Holdsclaw. Incidentally, she has had her jersey number retired at her college and has even had a street named after her in Tennessee.

19. Kenyon Martin

20. Jason Kidd, along with Grant Hill. Through the end of the 20th century, there were two other sets of co-winners for that trophy. The other co-honorees were Dave Cowens with Geoff Petrie in 1970–1971, and Elton Brand who shared with Steve Francis in 1999–2000. In the 1999 draft, Brand and Francis were selected one-two overall.

21. Marcus Camby

22. Boston

23. Eight

24. Michael Olowokandi, Mike Bibby, Raef LaFrentz, Antawn Jamison, and Vince Carter

25. Lamar Odom

26. Ray Allen

27. Michael Adams, Gary Payton, and Baron Davis

28. Cynthia Cooper, during the first game of the 2000 season. She did it in the uniform of the Houston Comets, and did so versus the New York Liberty.

29. Sam Jones

30. 1982, with Louisiana Tech winning the title.

31. Kevin Garnett

32. Nick Van Exel (pronounced ex-ell, not ex-cel)

33. The Lady Vols of Tennessee. Under the direction of coach Patricia Summitt, the Lady Vols have won countless national titles and once breezed to a 39–0 slate during a season (in 1998, their third successive title and Summitt's sixth overall).

In March of 2005, during the NCAA Women's Tournament, 52-year old Pat Summitt broke Dean Smith's career victory record as the winningest college basketball coach of all-time. She won her 880th victory in the Lady Vols' 75–54 defeat of Purdue in the second round of the tourney. Her record then stood at a remarkable 880–171 to Smith's 879–254 when he called it quits after 36 years of handling the chalkboard and clipboard duties for the UNC Tar Heels (in 1997).

Shortly after her historic win, NCAA officials presented Summitt with the game ball and a plaque. Not only that, Tennessee University officials announced that the court at Thompson-Boling Arena will now be named "The Summitt."

"Obviously," said a humble Summitt, "to be in the company with coach Smith, to think about all the people that were a part of these wins, I never thought I'd live this long."

34. Corey Maggette

35. 1. Glenn Robinson. 2. Pakman. 3. Bones. 4. Hammer. 5. Vince Carter. 6. Mark Madsen

36. Zach Randolph

37. Shawn Marion

38. Larry Bird

39. Stephon Marbury

40. Richard Hamilton

3 QUOTES

Basketball has produced some of the most interesting, offbeat, and humorous quotes around. Here's a sampling.

Marquette coach Al McGuire certainly knew the ins and outs of the game, but even he made mistakes in judgment on occasion. Listen to what he had to say about young Magic Johnson: "He'll suffer the first couple of years. They'll try to bring him too fast because they paid so much money. But they forget, he's only 20 years of age."

The reality of it was this—they didn't call him Magic for nothing. In his rookie season, 1979–1980, he averaged a very healthy 18.0 ppg and still managed to collar 7.7 rpg while handing out 7.3 apg to easily make it as a member of the All-Rookie team.

Johnson also won the MVP for the NBA Finals as his Lakers stormed to the championship. His numbers were even better the next year at 21.6 ppg, with exactly 8.6 for both rpg and apg.

For some reason or other, more than just one expert underestimated Magic Johnson's game a bit. When he was only a sophomore at Michigan State, his coach, Jud Heathcote critiqued, "He's so unselfish, players love to play with him. He'll never be a great scorer and doesn't have great physical strength or jumping ability, but he scores big points and controls the game under pressure. Quite simply, he's the best player in the open court. The closest thing to him is [Pete] Maravich. He'll be a great pro guard."

Well, aside from the comment about never being a great scorer, Heathcote was pretty much right on the money. For the record, Magic, who wasn't exactly physically weak either, wound up averaging 19.5 ppg over a long, illustrious career.

For years Calvin Murphy, who checked in at three inches under the six-foot mark, felt he had to prove himself to critics who judged him on size alone. They said he was clearly way too short to make it in the NBA. Murphy shook his head and said, "I know a lot of people can't accept that a 5' 9" man can play professional basketball well enough to be an All-Star. They just look at me and say, 'He's not supposed to be here.' In this league, images and reputation mean a lot, and you aren't supposed to be a good basketball player unless you're 6' 6" [or taller]."

Murphy, who would go on to become the Houston Rockets' all-time assists leader by his retirement, got to play in just one All-Star game (in 1979).

Murphy got the ultimate last word in when he was inducted into the Hall of Fame in 1992. He was certainly right when he said, "Take Kareem. If he was 6' 1", he would still play this game. Either you can play or you can't."

Charlie Just was the head coach of Bellarmine University in Louisville, Kentucky. When asked to comment on his squad's lack of experience, he joked, "We're so young, we've decided to dress only seven players on the road [games]. We're pretty confident the other five can dress themselves."

When Michael Jordan announced his retirement (actually, it was one of three times he called it quits) in 1999, Larry Bird was coaching the Indiana Pacers. A reporter asked Bird if Jordan was, indeed, the greatest NBA player of all-time. Bird smiled and said, "Is he the greatest? He's in the top two."

In December of 1998, the NBA was in the midst of a lockout. That is to say, the owners, as part of a labor struggle, locked the players out of their facilities. While there were no games to advertise, the Hornets, although far from being a winning team, ran a television commercial to appease their fans. It featured their mascot Hugo pushing a dust broom around an empty, dark Charlotte Coliseum. In the background Christmas music played, but otherwise there was silence. At the bottom of the screen these words scrolled by: "Look at the bright side. . . it's December and we're still tied with Chicago."

One time, Wilt Chamberlain looked back over some of the coaches he had known in the NBA. He commented on how some great players were far from great when it came to coaching. Dolph Schayes was, he said, a "great player who couldn't coach a lick. Nice guy. Too nice. But he couldn't coach. He was voted Coach of the Year and then he was fired a few weeks after that. Nobody else hired him, so I guess you'd have to say he got fired on merit."

Chamberlain said that his best all-round coach was Alex Hannum, pointing to the year he guided Philadelphia to a 68–13 season in 1966–1967. "We won 68 in a league that was twice as tough as the league was in 1971–1972 when Los Angeles was 69–13. There were only 10 teams in operation then [in '66–67] and all the talent was concentrated in those 10 teams."

Chamberlain, who was also on the '71–72 Lakers team, said that by that time there were 17 teams in the NBA "and almost that many in the ABA. The product was diluted." So, for leading such a team, Hannum got Chamberlain's nod of approval.

Coach Alex Hannum praised Chamberlain when a reporter asked him if he felt "The Stilt" was better than the then-active Kareem Abdul-Jabbar. Hannum replied thoughtfully, "Wilt was as talented as anyone in the history of the game. Kareem Abdul-Jabbar has the benefit of the latest technology and training and has a variety of skills maybe Wilt and Bill Russell didn't have. But, if Wilt was in his prime today, with the benefit of the training and the coaching now available, I suspect he would be better than Jabbar. Wilt was just incredible."

Shortly after Moses Malone won the MVP Award for a season in which he, among other things, led the NBA in rebounding, he was asked for his reaction. He replied, "I never thought I'd be the MVP or lead the league in rebounding." Then came his punch line, "But I got a lot of help from my teammates—they did a lot of missing."

All-time great center Nate Thurmond said that when a team drafts a player "if you're the number one guy, they'll give you three years [to pay dividends as a star]. They don't want to [wait that long], but they will." He said that often if a player doesn't click within that time frame "nobody else will want him."

Thurmond gave the example of Duke superstar Danny Ferry, who never attained such exalted status in the NBA. As Ferry entered his third year in the NBA, Thurmond commented, "He's going to have to show his stuff, or else. [He has] to show [he's] supposed to be a player, but I'm not giving up on him yet."

•

Some time after his playing days were over, Bill Russell signed a contract to appear in commercials for a telephone company. He was asked by the media how much money he'd make for his appearances. Russell grinned and replied, "Look for a rate hike."

When point guard Gilbert Arenas was a kid playing basketball video games where he could select which NBA player he could "be," he always went with Chris Mullin. He said he admired Mullin for his work ethic and he recognized Mullin as a fellow "gym rat." When Arenas showed up for a practice session with his Golden State Warriors, he was delighted to see Mullin, the Warriors Special Assistant, waiting there for him, ready to put him through a workout.

"Chris's presence has helped me out so much; it helps me stay focused," said Arenas. "He put me through one drill that was so hard, it was all this movement, running to half-court, shooting threes, then running back to half-court. And afterward he said that was just warm-ups."

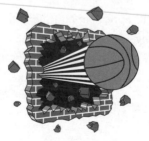

The year Wilt Chamberlain averaged 50+ ppg took a lot out of him. As he put it, "It completely wore me out." Then he added, quite correctly, "But I seem to play pretty well when I'm all worn out." He went on to say that the night he scored his 100 points against New York he had gone sleepless "for at least 30 hours."

On another occasion, he pondered that miraculous season in a different light. "When I look back on that season, I can't even believe it myself. How many players have even scored 50 points in a game in the NBA? Not many, I can tell you that. But I averaged scoring 50, which was way too much. If I had it to do over again, I would have settled for maybe 40, because after you score [on average] 50, they expect you to score 60 the next year."

When he was in his early years in the NBA, Kareem-Abdul Jabbar was often labeled as being unemotional—early critics said he gave the impression that he wasn't hustling, that he wasn't really "into" his games. It was almost, they contended, as if he really didn't care.

He responded to such charges in the era before he was hooked up as a teammate of Magic Johnson. "If I were to be like everyone else, it would be artificial because that's not the way I am. When a lion makes a kill, it doesn't growl or roar. . . [it's just business as usual]. This is just the way my personality has expressed itself all my life. It doesn't mean I'm not all worked up inside. It doesn't mean I don't care or I'm not trying."

When John Salley, now a television personality, used to play alongside Orlando Woolridge as members of the Pistons, Salley loved to tease his teammate about his lack of defensive skills. In other words, in the slang of basketball, Salley felt his buddy didn't play much "D." He once observed, "There's a 'D' in Woolridge, but it's silent."

When Pat Williams was the general manager of the Orlando Magic, he often came up with clever comments and quips. For instance, when he learned that Los Angeles Clippers center Benoit Benjamin had reported to camp around 30 pounds heavier than he had the previous season, Williams joked, "Benoit has given new meaning to the term expansion player."

•

Oscar Robertson's pick as the best player moving into the 21st century was Kobe Bryant. In his book, *The Big O*, Robertson stated Bryant, who has both size and speed, can do it all. "He makes the pass, the block, gets the rebound, gets out and gets the tempo up."

Alonzo Mourning spoke of how difficult it is playing the center position in the NBA, saying that being tough "comes with the territory. The position I play is an aggressive position—'bows [elbows] flying, people pushing, barking, you're all up in people's faces... It's not too pleasant down there in the hole. That's why only a select few play down there... very rarely do you find people that want to go down there and put up with that night in and night out. And I'm one of the select few who likes to do it."

Mourning went on to say effective centers cannot be frightened. "Intimidation is just a word. I look at it this way—I played against Patrick [Ewing] and Dikembe [Mutombo] for four summers straight in college [Georgetown], and I'm thinking, 'If I can play against those guys, I can play against anyone who steps on the floor.' So, intimidation? That's not even in my vocabulary."

When head coach Bobby Knight was at Indiana he was widely known for his wins and his fiery temper. One time, the Indiana football coach recalled a conversation he had with Knight about football's legendary Paul Brown. He began, "I was telling Knight how I'm really looking forward to getting into heaven and telling coach Brown how much I feel about him and appreciate all he did for football. So coach Knight right away pipes up and says, 'Well, what if he's not in heaven?' I said, 'Well then, I guess I'll let you tell him.'"

John Gabriel was a scout for the Orlando Magic when Luc Longley was playing his college ball at New Mexico. Gabriel teased, "One minute Longley plays like [all-time great] Bill Walton. Other times he plays like John Boy Walton."

Chicago Bulls Assistant Coach John Bach had many opportunities to study the great Michael Jordan. Bach was amazed by Jordan's ability and felt that when it came to pulling out late victories, Jordan was unsurpassed. Bach observed, "I always felt that Michael was ordained to do things, especially [late in the game] . . ."

He added that Jordan had the ability to attack "the basket with a destructive urge that everybody—his teammates, opponents, even the refs—had to respect. He was inspired in ways other players hardly ever are. I'm convinced that's why he was rewarded with such unusual success late in so many games."

Jerry West came up with a great, colorful quote concerning prolific scorer George Gervin. "You don't stop Gervin," noted West. "You just hope his arm gets tired after 40 shots."

Gervin, famous for his finger roll shot and for his shooting long bombs from "downtown," was a 6' 7" forward but could shoot like a guard. As a matter of fact, he hit the 40-point plateau 64 times during his NBA career.

Earl "The Pearl" Monroe was so creative when he had a basketball in his hands, defenders were left perplexed. He possessed more "moves" than a Broadway choreographer. Monroe once observed, "If I don't know [what I'm going to do with the ball], I'm quite sure the guy guarding me doesn't know either."

As the head coach of the Atlanta Hawks, Bob Weiss encountered an odd but funny situation. A rookie forward by the name of Trevor Wilson was on the Hawks' injured list. That didn't stop him, however, from bolting the team without notifying his coach. As it turned out, Wilson had left the United States to play ball for a team in Italy.

Weiss, shaking his head, said of Wilson, "I've had guys not show up. I've had guys forget the plays. I've had guys miss the bus. But I've never had a guy in the wrong country."

•

Jerry Sloan was known for his rugged, in-your-face defense throughout his playing days (1965–1976). With that in mind, Weiss set head coach Sloan up for a hard-hitting punch line. "In your prime," he said to Sloan, "you would have stopped Michael Jordan. Of course, in your prime, Jordan would have been 12 years old."

One NBA announcer marveled at Larry Bird's shooting touch, saying that the Celtic star, "just throws the ball in the air and God moves the basket underneath it." It must have seemed that way, as if Bird never missed. In reality, he shot almost exactly .500 for his field-goal percentage and clicked on almost 90% of his free throws.

Charles Barkley was famous for a whole lot of things, but modesty was never one of those things. By just his fourth season in the league, he had doubled his rookie scoring output, leapfrogging from 14.0 ppg to 28.3. He was once quoted as saying, "There will never be another player like me. I'm the ninth wonder of the world."

Longtime NBA coach Bill Fitch was a bit sarcastic when asked to evaluate the announcing skills of chatterbox Dick Vitale of ESPN. Fitch commented, "The last time Vitale said anything that made sense was when the doctor slapped him on the behind."

When Coach Mike Krzyzewski was hired by Duke University, he was not a high-profile name. While Duke fans would come to love and respect this legend, at first their reaction was more of a "Coach who?" situation. The average fan back then could neither pronounce his name nor spell it. Further, the Duke student newspaper wrote about Krzyzewski's hiring, adding in a headline, "THIS IS NOT A TYPO."

It didn't ruffle Krzyzewski at all. When he met the media for the first time on the Duke campus, he joked, "The last name is K-R-Z-Y-Z-E-W-S-K-I, and if you think that's bad, you should have seen what it was before I changed it." Before long everyone simply called him Coach K.

Prior to capturing the NCAA title in 1991, Coach K's Duke squad had played in four of the five previous Final Fours. Each time the team came up empty. One critic wryly commented, "Did you hear about the round of golf that Kyzyzewski played? He quit after 14 holes—didn't want to play the final four."

Danny Ainge was a feisty player during his college and NBA careers. When he first joined the Portland Trail Blazers, his new teammate, Jerome Kersey, gave Ainge a left-handed compliment. Saying he had changed his opinion of Ainge, Kersey stated, "He's not as dirty as we thought he was."

Ainge once commented, "I have this reputation as a complainer." He paused, setting up the punch line. "Actually, I'm a whiner, not a complainer."

Nate Thurmond was once asked to critique the play of Cavalier point guard Mark Price. Thurmond said, "He's outstanding–the only criticism I have is he plays with too much enthusiasm. Don't throw yourself up against a piece of wood, the floor is going to win."

Thurmond compared Price's aggressiveness to that of Larry Bird, but added Bird may have lost a year or two off his career by throwing his body to the floor so often. As Thurmond put it, "All-out hustle, especially when you first come into the league is fine; but [a player] must make up his mind sometimes, 'I can't get that ball.'"

Thurmond also noted that for a team to be successful they need to have more than just one star. He gave the example of former Cavs forward Larry Nance, calling him a "steady player. He adds so much [to a team] with his play and leadership. He works hard and he's a smart player. You need a solid player, a role player, an elder statesman."

After coaching for many a year at North Carolina State, Jim Valvano became a television commentator. One assignment had him traveling to Italy with Villanova coach Rollie Masimino and Lou Carnesecca of St. John's. Valvano later told of his adventures abroad. "Lou speaks fluent Italian and Rollie thinks he does. One night in a restaurant, Rollie decides to order for us. The waiter came back with three umbrellas."

Scott Hastings was hardly an NBA superstar, but when it came to having the ability to keep things loose and not take himself too seriously, he did just fine. One night in Cleveland when he ran off the court as the buzzer went off to end the first half, a fan shouted at him, "Hastings, you're a stiff." Without missing a beat, Hastings came back with, "Yeah, but I'm a rich stiff."

Another time Hastings, then with Denver, made one more biting joke at his own expense when he appeared on David Letterman's T.V. show. He began, "Every night when you lay your head on the pillow you say, 'I'm one of 300.'" He was referring to the fact that then only about 300 men were able to make it to the NBA. Hastings then added, "Of course, 50 of us stink really bad."

Hastings was acquired from the Hawks by the Miami Heat in the expansion draft. He reported to camp and gazed around only to see rejects from other teams, possible prospects, and unfamiliar faces. He later spoke with a friend and was perhaps only partially joking when he said, "I'm worried. I think I'm the best guy here."

Once, the public relations department at the University of North Carolina was working on their new media guide. When it came to commenting on their arch rivals, the Duke Blue Devils, they managed to get a dig in by labeling Duke the place "where Lefty Driesell was taught English and Richard Nixon studied law."

•

When asked if his lack of height—he stood only 5' 9"—was a big problem throughout his basketball career, Calvin Murphy put a different spin on the question. "Not at all," he began. "First of all, the average American is 5' 9". I'm the normal one in this league." When one thinks about it, he had a point—after all, how many people who stand 6' 9" and taller are typically seen walking down the streets of any town in the United States?

•

An "oops" award should have gone to the next quote. Doug West, after his Minnesota Timberwolves had mishandled the ball in a very sloppy contest, stated, "We threw it around like a hot tomato."

Jerry Tarkanian entered the NBA coaching ranks in 1992 with a terrifically successful college background, winning 84% of his games. In the NBA, though, the 62-year-old "Shark" wound up losing more games in less than two months than he had over his last three full seasons at the University of Nevada at Las Vegas. There he had guided the Runnin' Rebels to glistening records of 35–5, 34–1, and 26–2.

Tarkanian posted a ledger of 9–11 before he retired from the Spurs, announcing, "I'll never coach again. . . I probably ought to be out watering flowers."

Michael Adams was a low third-round draft pick back in 1985, the 66th overall selection in the NBA that year. It took him three seasons, playing for three different teams before he began to shine. Prior to that, he had struggled enormously. As Marty Blake put it, "Adams got cut more times than Swiss cheese."

Charles Barkley was a teammate of Danny Ainge, a fine jump shooter who loved to put the ball up. Grinning broadly, Barkley spoke of his statistics and commented, "When I want an assist, I throw the ball to Ainge because I don't have to worry about him passing it off."

Pete Newell, famous for working with and vastly improving big men, said of Hakeem Olajuwon, "He has, without a doubt, the quickest feet and the greatest ability to create a shot with those quick feet of anybody I've ever seen."

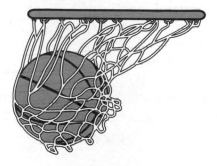

After Larry Bird called it quits, his Celtics felt an immediate drop off, starting the Bird-less Era with a miserable 2–8 record. Robert Parish, Boston's center, muttered, "It doesn't get much worse than that, and if it does, I don't want to see it."

The Celtics honored Bird with a special retirement ceremony that ran well over two hours. When fellow great Celtic star Kevin McHale was asked if he and Parish could expect the same type of celebration, McHale quipped, "I told Robert we'll probably get ours during a 20-second timeout."

Bird deserved his recognition. Of the first 60 times a Boston player registered a triple-double, Parish had achieved one such feat while Bird accounted for the other 59 times.

Wes Unseld was asked if 6' 10" rookie Tom Gugliotta reminded him of Larry Bird, Unseld cracked a smile and responded, "Big Bird is more like it."

Going into March of the 1992–1993 season, the Dallas Mavs had followed a pattern of being able to win only one game per month. Portland's Buck Williams was asked why teams would still hustle and play hard versus the woeful Mavs. He deadpanned, "You don't want to be their win for March."

●

Bill Sharman took over as the head coach of the Los Angeles Lakers in 1971. He convinced Wilt Chamberlain to focus on his rebounding and shot blocking, and not dwell so much on scoring. At first Chamberlain balked, but in the end it worked out well for the team. Again, though, his immediate reaction was to carp that asking him not to score was like "asking Babe Ruth not to hit home runs."

Elvin Hayes emphasized that no man could stop the mighty Wilt Chamberlain. Hayes gushed, "When I played him, I kept this foremost in my mind: don't make him mad."

The 1978–1979 playoff series between Denver and Los Angeles got pretty heated. When asked just how rough it was out on the court, David Thompson replied, only half-jokingly, "All I know is that I got more stitches than free throws."

Some pampered, highly paid athletes mumble and grumble about how tough their life is or complain about the intense pressure of their occupation. Shaquille O'Neal put sports in a proper perspective when he stated, "Pressure is when you go home and you don't know where your next meal is coming from." He went on to say, "I have no pressure. I just go out, play hard, and hopefully have a good game."

When O'Neal played his first NBA game, the opposing center was Rony Seikaly, who quickly put this perspective on Shaq: "There is no doubt he's going to be a monster. He palms the ball like a grapefruit. He's as big as Mark Eaton and seven times as quick. And he's only 20 years old—give me a break!"

During a particularly long losing streak, Cleveland Cavs coach Bill Fitch confessed that it was tough for him to come up with something positive to tell his struggling players. With so many things going wrong, Fitch reasoned there wasn't "much to praise. What am I going to say, 'Way to shower, kid,' or 'Nice sweating, buddy.'"

Kevin Loughery was the New York Nets coach when they went through some hard times. In the middle of losing their 13th game in a row, Loughery got on refs Earl Strom and Walter Rooney for a call that they had made. He shouted, "Hey, you guys are worse than we are."

Rick Morissey was writing a piece for the *Chicago Tribune* about Yao Ming when it appeared there was a chance Ming would play in the NBA. Morrisey wrote, "Yao is beefier than Manute Bol, but so is asparagus."

When Charles Barkley teamed with Rick Mahorn in Philadelphia, it gave the 76'ers a one-two "punch" of players who were notorious for their tempers and for numerous ejections, which inevitably followed their tantrums. At one point they discussed the idea of donating $3,000 every time one of them was kicked out of a game. However, after some thought, Barkley quipped, "We were going to donate the money to the homeless, but they would have had better houses than we have."

Upon unveiling a new model of his sneakers, Barkley joked, "These are my new shoes. They're good shoes. They won't make you rich like me, they won't make you rebound like me, they definitely won't make you handsome like me. They'll only make you have shoes like me. That's it."

Michael Jordan has spoken many a word of wisdom. Here's a sample of several such quotes:

1. "I can accept failure, but I can't accept not trying."

2. "I never looked at the consequences of missing a big shot . . . when you think about the consequences you always think of a negative result."

3. "I've always believed that if you put in the work, the results will come. I don't do things half-heartedly. Because I know if I do, then I can expect half-hearted results."

4. "I've missed more than 9,000 shots in my career. I've lost almost 300 games. Twenty-six times, I've been trusted to take the game winning shot and missed. I've failed over and over and over again in my life. And that is why I succeed."

4 PIONEERS OF THE GAME AND OTHER INTERESTING FACTS

Here are some interesting facts and anecdotes about teams and players who have impacted the rules of the game or contributed in one way or another to basketball's rich history. There are also stories about surprising draft pick sleepers and those players whose numbers have been retired.

The first seven-foot player in basketball is hardly a big name for most of today's fans, but Bob Kurland, nicknamed "Foothills," shocked college fans in the early to mid-1940s with his stature and ability.

Kurland is credited as being the first player to dunk the ball, yet he said he felt his height was a disadvantage in a way. "College coaches didn't want to take the time to develop tall boys like me," he explained. "The six-footers were faster and more poised."

When he was 13 years old, Kurland stood at a towering 6' 6" but was uncoordinated. He didn't even play basketball until he was in high school. By his college days, however, he could, for example, stand near the basket, jump ever so slightly, and swat the ball away from offensive players time and time again. As a matter of fact, back then he was even permitted to block the ball as it flew downward, heading right for the hoop, giving him a huge advantage over smaller players.

Kurland did not make an immediate impact as a college freshman in 1942–1943, but people took notice of his goaltending technique. The next season, NCAA officials studied his defensive strategy carefully and mulled over its legality.

After Kurland's sophomore season, a rule was drawn up making it illegal to touch the ball on its downward path. The penalty for violating the rule was simple—goaltending would be called and the basket would automatically count. Fans predicted that would be the end of Kurland's career, but he went on to enjoy a fine career and was a three-time All-American.

After Kurland's college days were over, there were pro contract offers, the best being a two-year, $30,000 deal, good money back then, but he elected to remain an amateur. "When I got out of college," he explained, "pro basketball wasn't nearly as attractive as it is now."

Kurland was and wasn't the game's first seven-footer. During his college days at Oklahoma A & M, his coach, the legendary Hank Iba, listed Kurland as being exactly seven feet tall. However, according to one report, Kurland himself (long after his playing days were over) stated that Iba had "stretched me an inch and a half because he figured the idea of a seven-foot basketball player would capture the imagination of the fans. And it did."

The practice of falsely listing the height of basketball players continues today at nearly every level of play.

In the 1941–1942 college season, the West Texas State team gained fame. It was nicknamed the "World's Tallest Team" because the average height of the starting five was 6' 6½". While that may have been impressive back then, by the 1980s there were ballplayers such as Magic Johnson who could run the point guard position at 6' 6" or better; Johnson went 6' 9" and could go inside with the ball just as easily as he could roam outside.

From time to time, rule makers find it necessary to create a change, making conditions difficult for big men to control the game.

When Lew Alcindor left high school and entered the world of college basketball at UCLA, he quickly dominated. Soon the NCAA banned the dunk shot, but the 7' 2" Alcindor adapted quite easily. Typically, he'd go up for what could have been an easy dunk and would then merely drop the ball, while keeping his hands outside the circumference of the rim, into the hoop.

In some respects, the rule actually helped Alcindor. Instead of becoming a one-dimensional dunking machine, he developed a nice touch around the hoop. That included, of course, his awesome skyhook, a shot requiring much more finesse than a dunk. It became a deadly and dependable weapon that nobody could defense (or outlaw).

The no-dunk ban lasted nine years, being lifted for the 1976–1977 season.

The area on the floor where an offensive player is allowed to enter, but stay for no more than three seconds, is known as the *lane*. It extends from the baseline to the free throw circle. Players line up around its perimeter while free throws are being attempted. Nowadays it's painted differently than the rest of the court, so it has been nicknamed "the paint."

At one time the lane actually looked like the name writers gave it long ago, the key. Experts say it was widened due to the impact of 6' 10½" George Mikan, an NBA superstar. The lane was only six feet wide when Mikan began his career, and it soon became clear that working inside such a small area gave Mikan the advantage of stationing himself a mere hop and a jump away from an easy score.

In college ball, the change from six feet to twelve took place prior to the 1955–1956 season, the year Chamberlain came on the scene as a freshman. Once again, the rule makers tried to minimize the strengths of big men.

Currently the lane resembles a wide rectangle and is now 16 feet wide, so it's not quite so easy for big men to stand, or "camp out," near the basket any more.

The NBA, at one time, banned the dunk—the most crowd-pleasing shot of all—for a while due to Wilt Chamberlain. Ultimately, nothing succeeded at slowing him down, as he led the league in scoring in each of his first seven years in the NBA.

Famous Shots

Writer Richard Levin came up with a list of shots that were made famous by top players in NBA history. He began by calling the skyhook of Kareem Abdul-Jabber a shot that "literally floats like a butterfly and in many respects stings like a bee. It is the ultimate offensive weapon in basketball, an indefensible, unstoppable shot that brings opponents to their knees in both reverence and despair."

Levin estimated that one season about half of all Kareem's shots were skyhooks, a shot first developed in fourth grade, and one that became an almost sure bucket from 12 to 15 feet out.

Other shots Levin called to mind were Hank Luisetti's running one-handed shot, an innovation at the time he unveiled it; Denny Sailors's jump shot; the runner that Bob Cousy loved to throw up at the hoop; the two-handed overhead set shot of Dolph Schayes; Neil Johnston's hook; and the fadeaway that Wilt Chamberlain often employed.

Hank Luisetti's introduction of the one-hander truly was revolutionary. Until he came along, players shot from the outside with both hands on the ball. Players closer to the hoop tended to rely on lay-ups or hook shots.

Luisetti began to develop his new shot as a student at Galileo High School. "I don't know how I came to think of it," he said. "It just seemed to be the natural way to get the ball in the air." Later, when told his shot was too unorthodox to be acceptable, he scoffed. "If a guy can putt standing on his head, he's a good putter."

Luisetti's point was really well taken during the 1937–1938 season when his Stanford team met up with a strong Duquesne squad at a neutral court in Cleveland. With his teammates urging him to shot the ball often, Luisetti set a record, becoming the first college player ever to pour in 50 points in a game. He did so en route to a 92–27 rout. Luisetti nearly scored twice as many points as the entire Duquesne team. By the time Luisetti's college career was through, he had led Stanford to three straight Pacific Coast titles (1936–1938) and had gained All-American honors three times as well.

Perhaps the first truly great ball handler and man who gained fame for giving the ball up was Boston's Bob Cousy. When he retired, he had done something no man had ever done before; he led the NBA in playmaking eight times.

Prior to Cousy's entering the pros in 1950, the NBA was revamped, going from 17 teams to 11. At the end of a special dispersal draft, three teams were each to pick a player from a list of three players. Amazingly, none of the teams wanted Cousy, so they agreed to put the names of the players into a hat.

The Knicks reached in first and drafted Max Zaslofsky, who wound up ending his career with just over 1,000 assists. The Warriors pulled the name of Andy Phillips, a solid player who, in fact, led the NBA in assists twice. The Celtics then were "stuck" with Cousy.

Cousy would go on to guide Boston to six NBA titles, including five in a row, and wound up with almost 7,000 lifetime assists. He was a first-team All NBA selection ten times over his 13-year career.

At one time Steve Patterson, not the same one who made it to play in the NBA with the Cleveland Cavaliers, held the high school record for the longest field goal of all-time. When he played for McMinn Central High School in Etowah, Tennessee, he launched the ball at the distant basket. Even he had to be astonished when he saw it go through the net some 93 feet away. The shot occurred in a district tournament game in 1976.

•

David Robinson, known as the "Admiral," earned that nickname as a player at the Naval Academy. There he set a colossal 33 records and became the first Division I player to score more than 2,500 points, haul down over 1,300 rebounds, and shoot better than .600 from the field.

Charles Barkley called Robinson "the fastest big man I've ever played against." No wonder he was the number one draft pick in 1987.

SIBLING RIVALRY

Brent, Drew, and Jon Barry are brothers who all made it to the pros, with two of them (Drew and Jon) doing so via Georgia Tech.

A fourth brother, known as Scooter, played for Kansas' 1988 NCAA title team, and also saw professional action in the Continental Basketball Association and in France, Germany, and Spain, but never in the NBA.

From the 1997–1998 through the 1999–2000 season, all three Barrys were in the NBA.

When 23-year old Brent Price was drafted into the league, he joined his older sibling Mark, then 28. During their first game facing each other in the NBA, Mark "schooled" Brent, who had earlier baited his brother. "I told him I was going to 'get into his jock.' That was the wrong thing to say. He came out and busted a three and said, 'I thought you were going to get me.'"

Harvey and Horace Grant, born on the Fourth of July in 1965, were twins who were obviously alike in many ways, but Harvey was, at 6' 9" and 225 pounds, an inch shorter and some 20 pounds lighter than his brother was.

●

Dick and Tom Van Arsdale were also twins who both attended Indiana and wound up playing a long tenure in the NBA, including one year together for Phoenix.

●

Twins Jason and Jarron Collins played together at Stanford before both were drafted into the NBA. Jason, who stands 7' tall, began his pro career with the New Jersey Nets as their center.

Jarron, who is an inch shorter than his twin brother, is also a center who entered the league as a member of the Utah Jazz in 2001–2002, the same season his brother was drafted.

Among the flashier brother acts was the Dominique and Gerald Wilkins duo. Dominique had more sheer talent and went on to score over 26,000 points. Gerald was no slouch, though, and managed nearly 12,000 career markers.

•

Tim Hardaway broke into the NBA in 1989. After he had logged four seasons (then missed one) both he and his brother Anfernee, better known as "Penny," played at the same time in the league.

In that first season, 1994–1995, Tim averaged 20.1 points and "Penny" outdid his big brother slightly, at 20.9 ppg.

•

When Dan Schayes, son of Dolph, and Jon Barry suited up for the Bucks back in 1992, it marked the first time sons of two Basketball's Hall of Famers became teammates.

FATHER/SON COMBINATIONS

Father-son combinations have existed in the NBA. For example, take Butch and Jan Van Breda Koff. In this case the father, Butch, was probably a better coach than he was a player. Jan lasted much longer in the league as a player (465 games) than his father did (175 contests). Jan wound up doing some NBA coaching, too.

●

Ernie Vandeweghe was a member of the New York Knicks, while his son Kiki enjoyed several years scoring over 20 ppg with the Nuggets and Trail Blazers.

Kiki's real name is Ernest Maurice Vandeweghe III. His mother Coleen, who gave birth to Kiki in Germany, is a former Miss America.

●

Grant Hill, a superstar before injuries hurt his offensive output, is not the son of a former NBA player, but his father is former football great Calvin Hill, who starred mainly as a member of the Dallas Cowboys.

Pete Maravich is a big name from the annals of the NBA, but his father, named Press, also played the game at the professional level. He lasted from 1945 to 1947 for two teams in the old National Basketball League but hardly produced as his son would.

Press averaged 4.6 ppg over just 51 contests while his son, whose middle name was Press, went on to amass nearly 16,000 points, good for a 24.2 ppg average with a high of 31.1 in 1976–1977.

Another basketball legend and Hall of Famer, Bill Walton produced a son who made it to the pro level. Luke spent his rookie year, 2003–2004, with the Lakers after starring at Arizona.

Bill's brother Bruce made it to the pro level, too, but in the NFL as an offensive lineman for the Dallas Cowboys from 1973–1975.

Henry Bibby played at UCLA and enjoyed modest success in the NBA for nine seasons before becoming a college coach. His son Mike attended Arizona and was named the Pac-10 Player of the Year while also gaining First Team All-America status by the Associated Press.

In college, Mike averaged 17.2 ppg, 5.7 apg, and nearly two and a half steals per game as a sophomore in 1997–98. Perhaps the NBA's best shooting point guard by 2003, he has been known for years for canning many big shots in big games.

Henry's brother Jim was a big league pitcher who, in 1973 as a member of the Texas Rangers, threw a no-hitter versus Oakland. He also pitched a one-hitter and a two-hitter over his career.

All-time great Rick Barry is part of perhaps the greatest father-sons combinations ever. As mentioned, he sent three of his sons to the NBA (Jon, Drew, and Brent).

Draft Pick Sleepers and Pleasant Surprises

In the early days of the NBA draft, teams could continue to select players as long as they wanted, basically until the pool of potential pro players was empty.

In 1973, the draft still ran an interminable 20 rounds, but the following year the NBA declared 10 rounds was the limit. The trimming continued, and was down to seven rounds in 1985, to three in 1988, and as low as two by the next season.

Long ago, general managers had ample chances to unearth a late-round sleeper. While it was certainly true that players selected late seldom pay off, there have been exceptions, rare nuggets claimed by prospecting front offices:

Michael Cooper, known for his tenacious defensive prowess, was the 60th pick in 1978. He went on to give rivals fits with his in-your-jersey "D." Long-time foe Larry Bird called "Coop" the "toughest guy to guard me in the league." Cooper even managed to make first or second string All-Defense squads eight seasons in a row, with five of those honors being first-team trophies.

As a high school player, James Donaldson was hardly sought out by college scouts—even though he was quite an imposing figure. In fact, only two colleges offered him a scholarship. Later he became the NBA's 73rd draft pick and even then, his coach, Lenny Wilkens said, "When we drafted him, we knew he wasn't ready. We told him to go to Italy and play for a year." So, banished to Europe, Donaldson toiled hard and before too long was good enough to lead the NBA in field-goal percentage.

Marty Blake, the NBA's Director of Scouting for over 30 years now, found Donaldson's case quite interesting, commenting, "He was [already] 7', 205 pounds in college. He was a jump shooter from outside. He didn't like to rebound on days of the week that ended in the letter 'y.' Then he gained about 80 pounds. He's an exception to the rule that most guys that go overseas are not good enough to play in the NBA."

The 7' 4" looming hulk known as Mark Eaton is yet another unusual story. He was actually drafted out of junior college (Cypress) late in the 1979 draft. Although the pros showed interest, he decided to stay in school, transferring to UCLA.

Once at UCLA, Eaton mainly sat the bench, and when he did play, he put up paltry numbers: 1.9 ppg; .449 field goal percentage; 2.4 rpg; and a measly .409 free throw percentage—hardly the stuff of a future professional. He had just about given up on the game, taking a job as what had to be the world's tallest mechanic, before he was once again drafted—as the 72nd pick in 1982.

Eaton has a successful NBA career. At one point, only one man had ever swatted more shots than Eaton, and that man was Kareem Abdul-Jabbar. In addition, over a five-year span, Eaton led the league in blocked shots four times.

Pugnacious Bill Laimbeer was drafted just two spots away from being a fourth-round pick. The rugged center enjoyed his biggest success in Detroit using his strength (a rival said he was so strong he was a "WWF wrestler") and finesse (he was a deadeye from the free throw line and could sink outside shots with the best of them).

●

Sarunas Marciulionis was born on June 13th and always felt #13 was his lucky number. He chose that for his uniform number mainly because for three years in a row he was the final man cut from the 12-player Soviet national team. Thus, wearing #13 served as a reminder of his early struggles to stay in the game and succeed.

Marciulionis was a Lithuanian lefty, a member of the Soviet Union team that knocked off the USA squad in the 1988 Olympics, and a mid-sixth round choice in 1987 who stayed in the NBA for a steady seven seasons.

Frank Brikowski was sometimes referred to as "Brick," an unfortunate nickname for a basketball player. Still, this Penn State grad became a success story as well. Even though he was drafted in 1981 (third round), he saw no NBA action until 1984.

Brikowski explained his situation, "When you go up against a higher draft choice in camp, it's tough. You have to do things quick to impress the coach. Just look at the percentage of those guys who do make it, the numbers speak for themselves. I'm just happy to be in the NBA."

•

Spud Webb, who became a household name as the little guy (5' 7") who made it to the NBA, was not selected until the fourth round.

•

Unbelievably, a sixth-round pick did well in the pros. It was Mike Dunleavy, a man who once led the NBA in three-point shooting, went on to become an NBA coach, and is the father of another pro player, Mike, Jr.

Lenny Wilkens disagrees with people who feel coaches tended not to keep low draft picks. He commented, "In camp, you [do] give a fair look at everyone. You have to in order to maintain your credibility. You hand nobody a job; they've got to earn it. You're always looking for a surprise."

When the NBA later went to a two-round draft, Wilkens felt, "A problem now is it's tough getting players into camp. They want guarantees before they'll come, and you can't always do that."

Marty Blake, who drafted Wilkens in 1960, had this point of view: "Players are better off [with less rounds in the draft]. It's better now for players and teams. A guy who wasn't drafted is now free to try out with any team. They can pick and choose. A team can now bring in more players, not just the ones they drafted. There's a bigger pool."

During the NBA's infancy, many teams had trouble drawing large crowds. To combat this troubling situation, the league's draft included what was known as territorial picks. Prior to the official opening of the draft, a team was permitted to surrender its first-round pick if they wanted to instead choose a player from the team's immediate geographic area.

The *Official NBA Encyclopedia* lists the example of Jerry Lucas, who played for Ohio State. He was so popular throughout the Buckeye State that the Cincinnati Royals gladly gave up their first pick to grab the talented Lucas. The move paid off immediately as fans flocked to watch the man who was destined to enter the NBA's Hall of Fame in 1979.

The practice of picking players from the team's area was discontinued after the 1965 draft.

When any established league gets challenged by a new, upstart league, there is a tendency (usually justified) to look upon the new organization as inferior. In basketball, the ABA came on the scene as a rival to the NBA. It started to compete against the established NBA on Friday the 13th in October of 1967.

While the ABA eventually ceased to exist, with the exception of several teams that were merged into the NBA, it is noteworthy that ABA teams did play exhibition games versus the NBA. Further, they actually won more contests than the "veteran" league by a 79–76 margin.

In those games, the red, white, and blue ball used by the ABA was put in use but only for one half. Likewise, the three-point shot and the 30-second shot clock, both ABA innovations, were in force for one half. The teams then used the NBA guidelines and rules for the other half of the contest.

The WNBA was born in 1996 when 29 NBA teams agreed
to sponsor a professional league for women. The league,
under the guidance of their first president, Val Ackerman,
decided to play their games during the summer.

Actual play began the following year with an
eight-team league. Further, just three years later the league
had doubled to 16 squads.

The first WNBA regular season contest matched New York
and Los Angeles and drew a throng of 14,284 fans back on
June 21st of 1997. By its second year of existence, the league
had maintained an average crowd of over 10,000 spectators
per game.

Shaquille isn't the NBA's only O'Neal. Jermaine has done quite well for himself, too. He was one of three players to average 20+ points and 10+ rebounds per game in 2002–2003, when he averaged a career-best 20.8 ppg and 10.3 rpg for the Indiana Pacers.

Jermaine O'Neal was voted the NBA's Most Improved Player in 2001–2002, not too many years after making his NBA debut, which he did at the age of 18 years, 1 month, and 22 days old. That made him then the youngest player in NBA history.

What's In a Number?

Normally, when a player has his uniform number retired it is because he was a dynamo on the court, a true star. However, in Boston, where they traditionally have more retired jerseys than any other NBA team, they honored a man who owned a career average of just 6.2 ppg. Jim Loscutoff wore the Celtic green and white from 1955–1964, scoring a total of 3,177 points, the lowest total of any man with a retired jersey in the entire league.

Loscutoff was honored, said a Celtics public relations worker because, "He was a member of seven championship teams." Interestingly, the team did not retire his number, 18, but a jersey with the nickname "LOSCY" adorning it. They made that decision because the team realized they would later retire the #18 worn by Dave Cowens, who was an active player at the time of Loscutoff's honor.

One seemingly odd decision to honor a player occurred in Cleveland when the Cavaliers decided to retire Nate Thurmond's #42. Thurmond was certainly a great player, but he spent only a portion of his career in the Cavs uniform. He explained, though, that it was "a matter of timing. I think I made an impact, plus the fact that I'm from the area [Akron, Ohio]." When asked if a committee had selected him, he replied, "They don't need a committee. The owner knows and appreciates what I've done."

Thurmond was in the hearts of Cavs fans as a vital part of the emotional "miracle" season Cleveland had when they won their first division title ever.

Thurmond is one of only a few men to gain retired jersey commendations from two different franchises, the Cavs and Warriors. "With Golden State," he commented, "I think it was [more] deserved. I [was] there for a long time and did a lot for the organization."

Wilt Chamberlain also had his number retired by two teams, the two that he led to titles—the Philadelphia 76'ers and the Los Angeles Lakers. The same holds true for Oscar Robertson, honored by the Cincinnati Royals and Milwaukee Bucks, and Julius Erving, honored by the New Jersey Nets and the 76'ers.

•

Sometimes an established player will give up or even sell his number to the newcomer. When Drew Gooden came to the Cavs for the 2004–2005 season, he let it be known he wanted to wear #0. Jeff McInnis, who already "owned" that number, told Gooden he could have the "zero," but at a cost of around $25,000! Gooden vetoed that idea and asked for #90 instead.

•

Indiana Pacers swingman Ron Artest, perhaps the best one-on-one defender in the NBA, announced he'd wear #91 for the 2004–2005 season as somewhat of a tribute to Dennis Rodman who once wore that number and was a defensive specialist.

Growing up a Bulls fan, Artest also wore #23 for part of his career to honor Michael Jordan. He also said that before he quit the game he planned on switching his jersey number at least twice more. He said he'd do that so he could wear the numbers of several other Bulls from the past: Steve Kerr and John Paxson.

Rick Barry really wanted to keep his uniform number 24 when he arrived in Houston. He had worn that number since his high school days, so he and good ol' #24 went back a long ways. However, the Rocket who wore #24 was superstar Moses Malone, prompting Barry to comment, "I didn't think I was big enough to ask him to switch. So I will wear number two at home and number four on the road."

The Rockets public relations director observed, "As far as I know there is no precedent for an NBA player wearing two different numbers. But you may remember in the old days, high school and college players wore even numbers at home and odd numbers on the road."

That practice made it easier on the referees and scorekeepers to keep track of which player had committed a foul.

Referees would signal with their hands to indicate the number of the player who had just fouled another. They'd hold up, say, three fingers on one hand to indicate the tens unit of the uniform number and, for instance, five fingers on their other hand for the singles digit of the players' number. In this case, the jersey number would have been 35. That's why no high school player was permitted to wear a number higher than 55, which is, of course, the highest number a ref could indicate using two hands.

The first woman to dunk during a college level game was West Virginia's Georgann Wells. She managed this on December 21, 1984 versus Charleston.

•

It's not exactly a common sight in college to spot two seven-footers on the court at the same time. Certainly it happens more now than in the older days of the game. Still, fans of the Jacksonville Dolphins of the Artis Gilmore era (1970) were quite accustomed to watching two seven-footers play because that team had giant teammates. Gilmore, "The A Train" stood 7' 2", while Pembrook Burrows had to settle for being the shorter of the two men at an even 7'.

•

The very first player to compile 20,000+ points was Bob Pettit, averaging a sizzling 26.4 ppg over his career with 16.2 rpg thrown in the mix.

Pettit's greatest game ever had to be the time he pounded in 50 points as a member of the St. Louis Hawks in Game #7 of the 1958 NBA Finals. His performance, then a record for the Finals, helped stop a Boston Celtics run of championships.

Dave Cowens was one of those players who made it big in the NBA despite getting a late start playing the game. He said his days on the court didn't begin until his junior year in high school in Newport, Kentucky.

Much like other NBA players such as David Robinson, one factor in Cowens's success was a growth spurt. Cowens sprouted five inches over one summer, gave up his dreams of becoming a swimmer, and turned his attention to basketball.

Cowens, who broke in with the Boston Celtics in 1970–71, became the team's mainstay. He played for Boston for ten years, winning the championship twice. Finally, he capped off his career when he was voted into the basketball Hall of Fame in 1990.

The gutsy, fiery, undersized center, sometimes called "Big Red," produced a steady (17.6 ppg) scoring output while doing many facets of the game well.

Amare Stoudemire took the NBA Rookie of the Year Award as a 20-year-old. Even more amazing, he did not start playing basketball until he was 14 years old. In addition, he even missed his junior season of basketball because of transfer rules, and, boy, did this guy transfer. In all, he attended six different high schools before finishing his prep career at Cypress Creek High in Orlando, Florida.

The 6' 10" power forward goes by the nickname "STAT" for Standing Tall and Talented and is, according to the official NBA web site, "an enormous physical talent, who is often compared to a young Shawn Kemp, Karl Malone, or Moses Malone." The site praised Stoudemire for his "brute force and amazing quickness for someone his size."

•

Those men who played with or against Bob McAdoo readily nodded their heads in agreement when they heard John Havlicek proclaim that McAdoo was the "best pure shooter I've ever seen." Jerry West chipped in, "There isn't another big man in the NBA who has McAdoo's agility and scoring ability."

For McAdoo's 852-game career, despite being a 6' 9" forward, this man with a feathery touch from far outside shot a lofty .503 from the field.

By way of comparison, writer Jim O'Brien pointed out many big-name players, including guards, shot with way less accuracy than McAdoo did. For instance, Joe Fulks, a fellow Hall of Famer, shot only .302 lifetime. Guard Bill Sharman, uncanny at the free throw line, shot only .426 from the field for his career, and he was the man Red Auerbach once said "was the greatest shooter from the backcourt the game has ever seen." Bob Cousy hit a dismal .375 on all of his shots other than free throws.

Writer Bob Ryan said of McAdoo, "His awesome scoring prowess—he is at once a pure shooter and a scoring opportunist, a rare combination—seemingly dictates that an offense revolve around him. No greater shooter, at any size, has ever played the game."

Gail Goodrich spoke of how vital the passing game is in basketball. While many players worry about their scoring statistics, Goodrich noted that the fastest way to get the ball from Point A to Point B is passing. Goodrich said that when an open man is spotted, "You rely on your instincts, and if you have to stop and think, you might as well forget it, because, by the time you've made your decision, the opening [for the pass] has been closed."

Not only can a sweet pass lead directly to a bucket, earning the passer an assist, other good things can come from the passing game. "Just as soon as you make your pass, you ought to be moving. The principle is known in basketball as the pass and cut. Hit the open man, pass to him, then try to get open again yourself . . ."

CoCo Vandeweghe is destined to follow in the rich sports tradition of her family. The thirteen-year-old began to make headlines in 2005 for her tennis prowess. Her mother Tauna was a volleyball player and a swimmer in the 1976 Summer Olympics, and once more in 1984; her uncle Kiki is a former NBA player and, most recently, the general manager of the Denver Nuggets; and her grandfather is Ernie Vandeweghe, a former player for the New York Knicks.

CoCo stands 5' 10" and is said to possess quick reflexes. She already has a serve which tops out at over 100 miles per hour. Her mom commented, "She's surrounded by [sports] 24/7."

When she was a mere 12 years of age, CoCo defeated her Uncle Kiki in a tennis match. Actually, according to a newspaper account, she was "dominating the match when it had to be called early" so, in an agreement similar to street basketball's "ok, next basket wins," they finally stated that whoever won the next point would take the match. Kiki then aced her, but respectfully refused all attempts at a rematch. "He won't step on the court with me now," said CoCo.

Dee Brown was a collegiate star at Jacksonville in tropical Florida. When he was drafted into the NBA, it was by the Boston Celtics. When the first wicked snowstorm hit, Brown was totally unprepared for the wrath of a New England winter. He actually wound up using a kitchen spatula to clear his car's windshield of snow and ice. "It was all I had," he explained, grinning sheepishly.

Bob Dolgan of *The Plain Dealer* wrote of Tracy McGrady's incredible scoring binge in which he scored 13 points in the final 35 seconds of a game in which the Houston Rockets beat the San Antonio Spurs. McGrady hit a three-pointer to cut Houston's deficit to 76–71 with 35 seconds left on the clock. With just over 24 ticks left, he made a four-point play (hitting a trey, and then clicking on the free throw after being fouled). With 11.2 seconds remaining, he sank yet another "three" to cut the Spurs lead to two. Finally, after a quick turnover, McGrady hit yet another trey with 1.7 on the clock, finishing with 33 points in a simply stunning 81–80 victory.

The salaries of players from an earlier era were as puny as they are hard to believe when contrasted to today's paychecks. Neil Johnston was a fine player back in the 1950s, eventually becoming a member of the Hall of Fame. Wilt Chamberlain recalled that Johnston was "the only man outside me who ever led the league three years in scoring and rebounding. I don't think he made more than $12,000–13,000 during his pro career."

Nowadays, a player who is lightyears away from being a superstar might earn, on average, well over $13,000 for playing one quarter in a game. An extreme example illustrates how money matters have changed.

In 2004, Pau Gasol, an NBA import from Spain, signed a maximum six-year extension for $86 million. That means the Memphis power forward was slated to earn over $14 million per season, which breaks down to almost $175,000 per game or $43,699 for one quarter's play.

Having won the NBA's Rookie of the Year Award in 2001–2002 and having compiled a three-year scoring average of 18.5 ppg, his team felt the seven-foot-tall Gasol simply had to be signed to a long-term deal.

5 WHO AM I?

See if you can figure out which basketball player is being described. The answers are on pages 156–158.

1. I attended Georgetown, where I was a collegiate standout at the guard position. I went on to become a huge star with the Philadelphia 76ers. My trademark move is a lethal crossover dribble that leaves many a defender behind as I breeze by them for countless lay-ups.

My 48 points in a game during the NBA Finals ranks as the sixth-best total ever for a Finals game. Furthermore, I have won the Rookie of the Year Award in 1997, league MVP in 2001, MVP of the 2001 All-Star Game, and a handful of scoring titles. Not bad for a, by NBA standards, small man (6' and 165 pounds).

Through 2003, I was one of only five guards to win the league's MVP, putting me in very elite company. Who am I? *The answer is on page 156.*

2. I played for 10 seasons in the NBA with five different teams (Milwaukee, Indiana, Orlando, Washington, and Philadelphia). I appeared in 600 games and averaged 6.5 apg, while shooting .889 from the free throw line, fourth best in NBA history.

I still hold the NBA record for most assists in a game with 30, set on December 30, 1990, as a member of the Orlando Magic. That same season, I was named the NBA's Most Improved Player, when I averaged a career-best 17.2 ppg and 8.4 apg.

Not only that, I was an All-American at Michigan State and have also enjoyed success as an NBA coach, most recently with the Chicago Bulls. Who am I? *The answer is on page 156.*

3. Only my relative inexperience stopped me from scoring 20 ppg as a rookie with the Toronto Raptors in 1998–1999, and even then I averaged 18.3. The next two years I exploded for 25.7, then 27.6 ppg. In college, I was everybody's All-American at the University of North Carolina, possessing athleticism galore. Only four men were drafted ahead of me in the 1998 draft. Who am I? *The answer is on page 156.*

4. I also spent time on the UNC court as a teammate of Vince Carter, but I left that campus earlier, entering the NBA in time for the 1995–1996 season. I was named First Team All-America by the Associated Press and Player of the Year by *Sports Illustrated* as a mere sophomore.

By 2000–2001, I ranked first in the NBA in total points and second in per game average (29.8), once scoring 57 points. I even led all NBA guards in 1996–97 with 63 blocked shots. Who am I? *The answer is on page 156.*

5. I was a multiple winner of the Slam Dunk Contest, known for my leaping ability, prowess on the offensive glass, and my fearlessness when it came to putting the "rock" up. I had a younger brother who made it to the NBA as well.

At 6' 8" tall, I played the forward spot. I was born in France and my real first name is Jacques. I played for Georgia, but left after three years to join the Atlanta Hawks, where I played for many seasons. Who am I? *The answer is on page 156.*

6. Although they listed me as being a 6' 7" center, in truth I was probably a good inch or two shorter, yet I went on to become a member of the Class of 1987 in basketball's Hall of Fame. One player called me the greatest 6' 6" center ever. Nowadays a center that small is unheard of—a virtual impossibility. Bill Walton admired my play because he said I gave up so much size and speed to opposing centers.

When it came to getting a rebound and starting a fast break with a quick, accurate, and, oftentimes, a very long outlet pass, I had few rivals. Walton observed, "It's too bad that his contribution to outlet passing is not carried into this current generation of players, who refuse to outlet the ball. . . No one just grabs it and snaps an outlet pass like [him]."

I spent my entire career with the Baltimore/Washington franchise, collecting nearly 14,000 lifetime rebounds. In my rookie year, 1968–1969, I only scored 13.8 ppg but my 18.2 rpg helped me win both the Rookie of the Year Award and MVP honors. Only Chamberlain and I had won both awards. Actually, we were also the only ones ever to gain MVP honors in our initial seasons. Who am I? *The answer is on page 156.*

7. I won the coveted NBA Finals MVP trophy in both 1999 and 2003 to become just the third player in history to earn Finals MVP honors in each of their first two trips to the Finals (joining Magic Johnson and Michael Jordan). I was also the regular season Most Valuable Player in 2001–02 and 2002–03.

I am also just the second player in NBA history to be named to both an All-NBA Team and an All-Defensive Team in each of my first six seasons as a pro— David Robinson was the first to do this. And since I also won the 1998 Rookie of the Year, it's safe to say I was an immediate impact player. Who am I? *The answer is on page 156.*

8. In the NBA, I wore Jersey number 31 for many years. As a member of the Indiana Pacers, I used to get into it with New York Knicks fans, especially a very vocal movie director who sat front row on the sidelines. In fact, New York was the site for one of my greatest feats ever—I lit up the scoreboard for 25 points in the final quarter of a playoff game in 1994.

As for my accomplishments, in 2003–2004, I moved by Charles Barkley for 14th place on the NBA's all-time career scoring list, finishing that season with over 24,305 lifetime points. That season I also went over 100 plateau for three-point field goals made for the 15th consecutive season, an NBA record, and became the all-time leader in three pointers with 2,464.

I've played in more games with the same team than all but two players in NBA history, John Stockton and Karl Malone of the Utah Jazz. Finally, I was a member of the gold medal-winning U.S. Olympic Basketball Team at the 1996 Summer Olympics in Atlanta. What's my name? *The answer is on page 156.*

9. I became a sensation when I entered the NBA in 2002—when a man stands 7' 6", he's bound to cause a stir. In my first two seasons in the league, I was named the starting center for the Western Conference All-Star team. Over that short span of time, I had already shot up to the third slot in Houston Rockets' history for career blocked shots per game.

I was voted *The Sporting News* Rookie of the Year by NBA executives while also earning unanimous NBA All-Rookie First Team honors in 2002–2003. One of my most interesting feats came when I posted the highest field-goal percentage in NBA history over a six-game stretch, making 31-of-35 shot attempts for an accuracy rate of 88.6 percent from November 9th through the 21st in 2002. Who am I? *The answer is on page 156.*

10. I was selected as one of the 50 Greatest Players in NBA History as part of the celebrations for the NBA's 50th anniversary in 1996, almost exactly 20 years after I was voted into the Hall of Fame. As a child, I had no basketball role model since my family couldn't afford to buy a television.

Years later, playing with an above-the-rim flair, I was an All-American at Seattle University. I made it to the NCAA Finals in 1958, where I won the MVP Award even though my team lost to Kentucky. The phrase "he has style, he has grace" could've been penned for me.

The Lakers, who then played in Minneapolis, made me the first overall choice in the 1958 NBA Draft. I was voted that season's Rookie of the Year and didn't stop there. When I finally hung up my sneakers, my 27.4 ppg average stood fourth best all-time, while my 13.5 rpg was second, among forwards, only to Bob Pettit. Who am I? *The answer is on page 156.*

11. I, too, am a part of the 50 Greatest Players in NBA History, but I played guard—although a pretty big one at 6' 7". I spent my campus days at the University of Houston, where our high-soaring team was nicknamed "Phi Slamma Jamma."

My NBA saga began in 1983 with Portland, although I ended my career back in Houston, this time with the Rockets. There I was reunited with my former college teammate, Hakeem Olajuwon. I helped the Rockets win their second straight title that season.

When it was all over, in addition to my 1992 Olympic gold medal and 10 All-Star selections, I was one of just three men to surpass the 20,000-point plateau with 6,000 or more rebounds and 3,000+ assists. Who am I? *The answer is on page 157.*

12. My highest scoring season was my third in the league, 2000–2001, when I broke out with a 24.9 ppg showing. By the end of the 2003–2004 season, I owned 182 games where I had thrown down 20+ points, hit for 30+ points 46 times, had 40 or more on five occasions, and topped the 50 plateau twice, doing that in back-to-back games in 2000.

I have been involved in some big trades during my NBA career, which began when I was selected after my junior season at the University of North Carolina. I originally went to the Toronto Raptors as their fourth pick overall in the 1998 NBA Draft. However, my draft rights traded were soon swapped to Golden State for the draft rights to Vince Carter and cash.

In 2003, I was peddled to the Dallas Mavericks along with Danny Fortson, Chris Mills, and Jiri Welsch in exchange for Evan Eschmeyer, Nick Van Exel, Avery Johnson, Popeye Jones, and Antoine Rigaudeau. Less than a year later, I was traded by the Mavs along with cash to the Washington Wizards in exchange for Jerry Stackhouse, Christian Laettner, and the draft rights to Devin Harris. Who am I? *The answer is on page 157.*

13. I am another ballplayer elected to the 50 Greatest Players in NBA History. I checked in at 6' 10" and had the defensive ability to clog the middle while oozing an aura of intimidation down low. Most experts say no man ever crashed the offensive boards better than me. I am a multi-year All-Star.

Not only did I draw a truckload of fouls, when I shot from the charity stripe I clicked on 77% of those shots—great for a big man. When I retired, no player had ever made more foul shots or collected more offensive rebounds than me.

When Rod Thorn was the Nets assistant coach, he said this about me: ". . . hard to box out because he's constantly moving around. With his quickness, any time he's near the basket he's got his hand on the ball."

Perhaps the biggest clue is this: I was the first man to make the jump from high school all the way up to the pro level.

I began my career in 1974 with Utah, but my highlight had to be winning it all with the 76'ers in 1983, although my three MVP trophies can't be ignored. Do you know who I am? *The answer is on page 157.*

14. In what was described as "one of the most successful jumps from high school to the NBA," I impressed fans and media alike by capturing the 2002–2003 NBA Rookie of the Year award at just 20 years of age. I was the ninth overall pick in the 2002 NBA Draft, and instantly helped turn around the struggling Suns.

I was named the NBA Western Conference's Rookie of the Month for January and April, the Suns' first monthly winner since way back in April of 1988 when Kevin Johnson was so honored.

In my initial season, I ranked seventh in the league with 3.1 offensive rebounds and 12th with 8.8 rpg. Back then, I also erupted for 38 points, the most ever in NBA history by a player making the jump from high school to the NBA in his rookie season, doing so in only my 31st game. Who am I? *The answer is on page 157.*

15. I was one of the first three women to sign a WNBA contract since I was a big-name college player and that helped promote the new women's league. I starred at the University of Connecticut. My initials are R.L. Who am I? *The answer is on page 157.*

16. I selected uniform number 0 because that was the number of minutes some people said I would average when I went to play my college ball at Arizona. They were dead wrong—I was good for 15.8 ppg over 70 games and two years for the Wildcats before entering the draft after my sophomore year. When I left the Arizona campus, I established myself as just the sixth player in school history to reach the 1,000-point plateau as a sophomore.

Although I was a 6' 3" shooting guard in college, I switched to running the show as a point guard with the Warriors as their number two draft pick.

My father is an actor who has appeared in several television commercials after enjoying a football career at the University of Miami, where he played halfback for the 1980 Hurricanes with Jim Kelly and Otis Anderson. Final clue: During my 2001–2002 rookie season, I was tied for the third highest single-game point total by any NBA rookie, trailing only two scoring sprees by Jason Richardson. Who am I? *The answer is on page 157.*

17. I coached the Bullets to an NBA title in 1977–1978, but learned a tough lesson in years to follow. I once commented, "Now I know what Vince Lombardi [famed NFL coach] meant. To get there is one thing. To stay there is tougher."

One of my star players, Elvin Hayes, observed this about me: "He demanded a lot of his players. He demanded a lot of himself. He gave us direction, and we followed it." Another huge star on that squad was center Wes Unseld, who said, "What we needed was an iron hand." And I guess that's just what I gave them en route to the championship.

It's a fact that I began my career as an unknown, with my only coaching experience being at the high school level and at Weber State. When I retired, I had chalked up more wins than almost any pro coach ever had—only four men owned more victories than me at that point. Who am I? *The answer is on page 157.*

18. I was one of the original three females to help launch the WNBA. Our catchy slogan for the league was, "We got next." On July 30th of 2002, I made history while playing against the Miami Sol as I became the first WNBA player to dunk in a game. That same season I was the MVP of the WNBA Championship and All-Star Game. My initials are L.L. Can you identify me? *The answer is on page 157.*

19. I am a 6' 3" player out of the University of Maryland who, in 2003–2004, joined Oscar Robertson, Magic Johnson, and Grant Hill as the only players in NBA history to average 15 points, five rebounds, and five assists in each of their first five seasons.

By that time, I already stood tall among Houston Rockets all-time greats, ranking second in career assists average, third in career steals average, fourth in triple-doubles, fifth in three-pointers made, and fifth in steals.

When I poured in a career-high 44 points with 11 assists vs. the Lakers during a 2003 contest, I became the first player in Rockets history to reach 40 points and 10 assists in a single contest.

Not only that, when I averaged 19.9 points, 6.9 rebounds, 6.5 assists, and a career-high 1.76 steals per game during the 2000–01 season, I made history as the first Rockets player and only the 18th player in NBA history to lead my team in total points, rebounds, and assists.

For a guard, I am a great rebounder. Additionally, I am the first man in the Rocket's history to amass 400 rebounds and 500 assists in the same season. I not only set my team's rookie record for assists in a season, I also became the first "freshman" in franchise history to win NBA Player of the Week, on January 24th in 2000. From all these clues, can you guess my identity? *The answer is on page 158.*

20. When I left college, there was a turf battle going on between the NBA and the new ABA. Both teams wanted me for my height (7' 2") and for my skills. The ABA won the bidding by dishing out a contract for $2.5 million, big bucks back then. In return, I won both the Rookie of the Year Award as well as the MVP plaque in my first year.

I spent my first five pro seasons with the Kentucky Colonels before joining the Chicago Bulls. From there, it was on to San Antonio, and I wound down my playing days with a short stint in Boston. Who am I? *The answer is on page 158.*

21. I entered the NBA in 2003 as the fifth overall pick, selected by the Miami Heat to play the point guard spot. This was a switch for me, as I normally had been the shooting guard. I now consider myself to be both a point and shooting guard, and that combo somehow works.

I did well right away in the NBA, scoring more than all but two fellow rookies at 16.2 ppg. Plus, only three rookies were more effective at dishing the ball off, as I posted 4.5 apg.

Born in 1982 in Chicago, I played at Marquette. I became an immediate favorite among card collectors who coveted my rookie card. My initials are D.W. Who am I? *The answer is on page 158.*

22. My first three years in the NBA were explosive, as I averaged 19.0, 20.2, then 19.4 ppg. Since then my scoring has tapered off, but I'm always good for around seven assists each time I take to the court.

I broke in with Toronto in 1995–1996 by way of the University of Arizona, but spent most of my career with Portland. I was selected as the 1995–96 Schick NBA Rookie of the Year, leading the Raptors with 19.0 ppg and 9.3 apg, which was the fifth best output in the NBA.

I recorded the first triple-double in Raptors history, with 20 points, 12 rebounds, and 11 assists, against Seattle on November 21, 1996. My initials are D.S. Name me. *The answer is on page 158.*

23. I am the third of the first three women to sign WNBA contracts, and have matching initials: S.S. I was selected as the 2003 WNBA Defensive Player of the Year, and have won two MVPs through 2004. Who am I?
The answer is on page 158.

Answers

1. Allen Iverson

2. Scott Skiles

3. Vince Carter

4. Jerry Stackhouse

5. Dominique Wilkins

6. Wes Unseld

7. Tim Duncan

8. Reggie Miller, the younger brother of another basketball star, Cheryl.

9. Yao Ming

10. Elgin Baylor

11. Clyde Drexler

12. Antawn Jamison

13. Moses Malone, a man, who according to Duke coach Mike Krzyzewski "went into a league where there were men. The [high school] guys who are leaving today are going into a much younger league. To do what Moses did was phenomenal, based on his background, the time and history. It's amazing what he has done."

14. Amare Stoudemire, a player whose childhood idol, Shaquille O'Neal, was so impressed with that he stated, "I've seen the future of the NBA and his name is Amare Stoudemire."

15. Rebecca Lobo

16. Gilbert Arenas

17. Dick Motta

18. Lisa Leslie of the Los Angeles Sparks. Incidentally, Leslie, who says the person she most admires is her mother, a cross country truck driver, once signed a modeling contract with a professional agency.

19. Steve Francis

20. Artis Gilmore

21. Dwayne Wade

22. Damon Stoudamire

23. Sheryl Swoopes, the first woman to have her own Nike basketball shoe named after her ("Air Swoopes").

6 NICKNAMES

There are many interesting and unusual nicknames for high school, college, and NBA teams and players. Let's see how many you're familar with.

Team Nicknames

Yuma High in Arizona go by the name Criminals. The reason stems from the fact that back in 1912 the school was transformed into a prison and a new school was erected. The next season, an opposing team teased the Yuma athletes, calling them criminals. The name stuck and, within four years, it became the official nickname of the school.

There's a poetic name in Blooming Prairie, Minnesota: the Awesome Blossoms. The team had once been known only as the Blossoms (due to the wildflowers that grew in the vicinity), but the students felt that wasn't too intimidating, so the Awesome part was tacked on.

Some more of the funniest and most interesting high school nicknames include the Poca Dots, for a West Virginia team; the Frankfort (Indiana) Hot Dogs; Bell Buckle (Tennessee) Webb Feet; the Monsters, fittingly from Gila, Arizona; and from Montana, the Belfry Bats.

In Philadelphia, a school named in honor of Thomas Edison took on the moniker of the Inventors.

The Brockton (Massachusetts) team is called the Boxers as a tribute to former heavyweight champ Rocky Marciano.

Many nicknames come from the animal world. There are teams known as the Hippos, Bloodhounds, Clams, Copperheads, Goats, Pandas, Tarantulas, Zebras, and one ideal name for basketball, the Kangaroos of Terryville, Connecticut. [*Source: John Pitts and Pamela Brown*]

Two nicknames of NBA teams don't make sense unless one knows his or her history. The Lakers, of course, are from Los Angeles, but what was the logic or reason behind this? After all, there are very few lakes in the L.A. area. However, that franchise actually began in 1947–1948 as the Minneapolis Lakers, and that does make sense. Minneapolis is situated in Minnesota, a state that proudly bears the nickname "The Land of 10,000 Lakes."

Then there's the perplexing case of the Utah Jazz. The solution to this nickname mystery is similar to that of the Lakers—Utah got their team via New Orleans. While jazz is certainly associated with New Orleans, which gave birth to the Jazz in 1974, Salt Lake City, Utah, isn't a jazzy kind of town. Still, for some reason, officials decided to retain the nickname when play began there for the 1979 season.

An ABA team had an interesting story involving its nicknames, and it had four of them. The New Orleans Buccaneers were charter members of the old league, born in 1967–1968. After spending the first three years of its infancy there, the team moved to Memphis, where they took on the name Pros.

The Pros weren't drawing enough fans from the Memphis area, so they wanted to expand their fan base to the surrounding area. They switched their nickname to the Tams and explained that the first three letters of that name stood for the three states they hoped to appeal to— Tennessee, where they would still be based, Arkansas, and Mississippi.

In their last year of existence, they became known as the Memphis Sounds, in honor of the great music scene in that city.

There were plans for the team to shift to Baltimore. Two nicknames had even been selected—first, the Hustlers, then the Claws, but the league died before the move was made.

●

Many of the WNBA teams' nicknames have a logical tie-in to the nicknames of their NBA "brothers." For instance, Utah's NBA team is called the Jazz, so the WNBA franchise went by Starzz, with the "double-Z" spelling.

More obvious were examples such as the Charlotte Sting for women and Hornets for the men; Miami Heat of the NBA and the WNBA's Sol (pertaining to the sun); the Washington Wizards and Mystics; Minnesota Timberwolves and Lynx; Orlando Magic and Miracle; and even the similar sounding and space-travel-themed Houston Rockets and Comets.

•

The Cleveland Rockers were named as a tie-in to that city's Rock and Roll Hall of Fame Museum.

Meanwhile, in a logical connection to the Statue of Liberty, a "lady" who has stood in the waters off New York City for decades, the Big Apple's WNBA team was nicknamed Liberty.

Player Nicknames

UCLA star Keith Wilkes went by the name "Silk."
Donald Watts, who joined the Seattle Supersonics in
1973, was known as "Slick," which was a description of
his hairless head and a tribute to his uncanny passing
and theft abilities. Terry Catledge, a first round pick
of the Philadelphia 76ers in 1985, was called "Cat Man."
Meanwhile, Greg Anderson liked his handle of
"Cadillac."

Lloyd B. Free liked his moniker "World" so much, he
actually had his name legally changed from Lloyd to
World—a reflection of his rather large ego. His middle
initial stood for absolutely nothing, except possibly a
play on words declaring him to "be free." The "World"
part was his way of boasting that he was better than,
say, All-American—he was All-World.

George Gervin was "The Iceman," earning the name because he was so calm and cool, even when under extreme pressure.

•

Walt Frazier was quite cool and dapper, wearing the most stylish of clothes, including velour hats, so he took on the name "Clyde" from the stylish title role of the movie *Bonnie and Clyde*.

•

The great Clyde Drexler went by "Clyde the Glide." Writers felt he was so smooth, it was as if he got around the court on skates, leaving defenders behind him.

•

As a tribute to Alex English's deadly shot, the Hall of Famer was sometimes called "Flick."

•

During his days on the Providence campus, Marvin Barnes, because of his rough and tumble ways, became known as "Bad New" Barnes. He had a reputation for being very undisciplined.

Due to his outstanding shot-blocking ability, the 7' 1"
Marvin Webster was dubbed "The Human Eraser."

Corliss Williamson, an intimidating figure, sometimes
went by the fearful name of "Big Nasty."

At 6' 7" and 225 pounds, the powerful Len Robinson was
simply known as "Truck."

One intimidating nickname was shared by two teammates, burly Mark Olberding and Dave Corzine (6' 11"
and 255 lbs.). Collectively they were known as "The
Bruise Brothers."

An obscure player by the name of Leslie Hunter was
sometimes called "Big Game" Hunter as an obvious play
on words.

Kentucky's Kenny Walker, who mainly played for the Knicks during his NBA tenure, quite naturally became "Sky" Walker in a "Star Wars" kind of tribute (not to be confused with another acrobatic jumper, James "Fly" Williams of the old ABA).

When Princeton star Bill Bradley signed a lucrative contract with the Knicks, he became known as "Dollar Bill." Bradley was an All-American, a Rhodes scholar, and a future politician who scored 2,503 points during his college days. That was the fourth highest total ever at that time.

Many Boston players had nicknames. Joseph White became "Jo Jo" during his long career, mainly with Boston, just as Celtics Tommy Heinsohn was "Ack-Ack."

Another Celtic great, John Havlicek, became "Hondo." Not only was that nickname alliterative, it also was a reference to (some say Havlicek look-alike) John Wayne, a strong leader type to be sure.

Larry Bird's nickname carried some well-deserved "boast" to it: "Larry Legend."

"Pistol Pete" Maravich concluded his career in a Celtics uniform and got his moniker for his love of shooting the ball.

Perhaps John Hargis liked to shoot more than Maravich, if that's possible—as Hargis was known as "Shotgun."

Bob "Butterbean" Love was not, as one might expect, overweight; he stood 6' 8" and checked in at 215 pounds.

Some nicknames involve food, such as the nicknames of Cedric "Cornbread" Maxwell and Rumeal Robinson, who answered to "Meal Time."

Back in the late 1940's, a 6' 9" player was considered pretty tall, earning William Henry the name "Big Bill."

Mel Turpin was (at 6' 11") a big man with an equally large reputation coming out of the University of Kentucky. He was so highly regarded, he was selected just three picks after Michael Jordan in the first round of the 1984 draft.

Due to various reasons, Turpin's pro career never panned out. His weight was a factor, as he was no doubt heavier than the 250 pounds listed in some sources. When he was with the Cleveland Cavaliers, his road uniform contained a lot of bright orange. That led someone to stick the nickname "The Great Pumpkin" on him. An even crueler name given to Turpin was "Dinner Bell Mel."

•

An alliterative nickname that tied in with one particularly flashy player belonged to Ron "Hollywood" Harper.

•

Billy "Kangaroo Kid" Cunningham, and "Jumping" Johnny Green naturally both got their nicknames for their magnificent "skying" ability.

Steve "The Franchise" Francis is a name that pays an ultimate compliment. "Franchise" refers to the fact that the entire team could be, or actually was, built around the man.

•

Nate Archibald went by "Tiny" due to his rather small frame (6' 1" and 160 lbs.). Some members of the media also dubbed him with the poetic title of "Nate the Skate."

•

Clearly some nicknames came about because they created fitting rhymes. Some included: guards "Downtown" Freddie Brown, Dean "The Dream" Memminger, and Earl "The Pearl" Monroe. Years after Monroe broke onto the scene, Dwayne Washington also went by "Pearl."

•

One player had a nickname that resulted in three rhymes. That title belonged to five-year veteran Bill "The Hill" McGill.

Many nicknames are so ingrained fans couldn't think of a given player's name without his nickname too. It was hard to say Wilt without adding "The Stilt" for Chamberlain, although many also called him "The Big Dipper."

Some people called Lakers great James Worthy "Big Game James" for his ability to excel in important contests.

NBA center Ronald Seikaly had Greek roots. While almost everyone called him Rony, some colorful writers would occasionally slip "The Greek Peak" in their prose to describe the 6' 11" center.

It may not have been an commonly used nickname, but Pervis Ellison was called "Never Nervous Pervis" at times.

Many fans didn't even know the real first names of men such as "Kiki" Vandeweghe (Ernest), "Happy" Hairston (Harold), "Sleepy" Floyd (Eric), or "Tree" Rollins (Wayne). The same holds true for Carlton "Scooter" McCray.

Perhaps Tyrone "Muggsy" Bogues should have also been named "Tiny," as he stood at a minuscule 5' 3"—unbelievably short by NBA standards. However, he compensated for his lack of height by his equally remarkable quickness.

That was also true of the waterbug-like "Spud" Webb, born with the first name of Anthony. In his case, the nickname came from his childhood when kids would tease him saying his head was as big as a Soviet satellite, known as sputnik—that name soon was altered to "Spud."

Julius Erving was called "Dr. J" so often, few fans even thought of him as Julius. The same held true for fellow-legend "Magic" Johnson, who was born Earvin.

Very few people called 6' 7" "Penny" Hardaway by his birth name, Anfernee. (His brother Tim, at a mere 6' tall, was sometimes called "The Bug.")

Many players had two-word nicknames. Michael Ray Richardson who was such a sweet scorer, he got a nickname that formerly belonged to a couple of great prizefighters, "Sugar Ray."

Rod Hundley became "Hot Rod" for his blazing scoring hand, the same nickname given to John Williams, who starred mainly for the Cleveland Cavaliers.

The explanation for Karl Malone's nickname "The Mailman" is simple: he delivers, coming though for his team time and time again.

174

Allen Iverson likes his nickname "The Answer," as it seems to say he is the answer to his team's prayers and needs. He even wears a sleeve on his elbow with his nickname written on it and one of his more than 20 tattoos features the words "The Answer" on his left arm.

Sherman "The General" Douglas, a positive stunner in Syracuse, deserved his nickname, since he was a general on the court as a point guard. Of course, since there really was a famous general with the first name of Douglas (MacArthur), the nickname took on the flavor of a pun, too.

Chuck Connors Person was also known as "The Rifleman," but not because he loved to shoot (which he did). Instead, his nickname was a logical extension of his first and middle names. There was an actor named Chuck Connors who played the role of *The Rifleman*, an old television western. Person's mother was a huge fan of the show and the actor who, by the way, played professional basketball for Rochester and Boston.

At times, Reggie Theus was called "Rush Street" Reggie after a famous street in Chicago where he played as a member of the Bulls.

•

Walter Davis was sleek and quick, so he became "The Greyhound."

•

The name "The Wizard" belonged to Gus Williams, who spent six great seasons with Seattle.

•

Oklahoma State's Bryant Reeves, who stood 7' tall, answered to "Big Country," while the 6' 9" Kevin Restani was "Big Bird."

•

Robert Parish had such a stony look on his face someone called him "The Chief" and that name stuck.

In a rare instance, two men took on a collective two-word nickname, "Twin Towers." In this case, it referred to a pair of Houston teammates, the 7' 4" Ralph Sampson and Hakeem Olajuwon, who stood 7' tall.

Olajuwon, who became only the third man in NBA history to record a "quadruple-double," also went by the "Nigerian Nightmare," as well as the respectful title of "Hakeem the Dream." This terrific center from Lagos, Nigeria, was the first man ever to have 2,000 or more blocked shots and steals. He retired as the all-time leader in blocks, with 3,830 to his credit.

Jerry West had even more nicknames than Olajuwon. He was known as "Mr. Clutch" and "Mr. Outside," but also had the colorful moniker of "Zeke from Cabin Creek." Writers said he hailed from a town by that name in West Virginia (actually, that was where his parents received their mail; he was born in Chelyan, West Virginia, a town with a listed population of a mere 500).

Dominique Wilkins has one of the longer nicknames in NBA history, "The Human Highlight Film," but he earned it with his acrobatic leaps and dazzling plays.

•

Charles Barkley gained the nickname the "Round Mound of Rebound" back in his college days at Auburn—it wasn't until much later that some took to calling him "Sir Charles." Hardly a greyhound of a basketball player at 6′ 6″ and about 275 pounds (later in his NBA career, his weight was listed at around 250), he somehow got the job done, pulling down tons of rebounds. By the time he retired, he owned 12,546 rebounds and over 23,000 points.

•

The 6′ 7″ and 240-pound Clarence Weatherspoon went by "Spoon" as well as "Baby Barkley."

•

"Fat" Lever didn't get that name due to his physique. The "Fat" part was a shortened version of his real first name, Lafayette.

"Campy" Russell acquired his nickname from his middle name, as he was born Michael Campanella Russell.

Dr. J wasn't the only player to make house calls. Darrell Griffith was once called "Dr. Dunkenstein," a name later shortened to "Dr. Dunk" in some circles (plus some called him "Chief Surgeon"). When he played at Louisville, his coach, Denny Crum said in utter disbelief, "Darrell does things no other human can possibly do."

Connie Hawkins, a player who skied high for a slew of dunks, was called "Hawk." He played in the old ABL and won that league's 1961–1962 MVP Award at the age of 19. A legend of the playgrounds of New York, when he signed with the ABA, he gave that upstart league a degree of respectability it had been sorely lacking.

●

Calling a player by his initials is hardly an imaginative nickname, but it's a fairly common theme in sports. Dennis Johnson was "D.J." to many a teammate. Notre Dame grad Adrian Dantley went by "A.D." Thurl Bailey only required one initial for his nickname; he went by "Big T." Ernie DiGregorio's last name was a tough one to pronounce, so he became "Ernie D." Xavier McDaniel gained the name of "X-Man."

●

Several superstars combined the word "big" with their first initial to form a respectful nickname. The most obvious were Elvin Hayes ("The Big E") and Oscar Robertson ("The Big O").

Boston's All-Star forward Kevin McHale was given the humorous nickname, "The Black Hole." The story goes that teammate Danny Ainge gave him the name because McHale loved to shoot from down low on the court so much that when you gave him the ball, it would "never come back out again," not unlike a black hole in outer space. Incidentally, McHale's fans even took on a name of their own, "McHale's Army," as a spoof of an old television show called *McHale's Navy*.

When high-flying Larry Nance won the NBA's first Slam Dunk Contest, the media tried to pin a colorful label on him. They tried such crazy ones as "Mr. Slambassador," "Flash Nance" as a takeoff of the movie title Flash Dance, and even the "High-Atolla of Slam-olla." Mercifully, none of the names stuck.

Derrick Chievous went by the name "Band-Aid" because during his playing days he would always wear one, even when he didn't need it. For him it was simply a ritual, one, they say, that began when he was in junior high school. It seems that one day he did need a Band-Aid to cover a cut above his eye, and in a game that day he rained down some 45 points. That outing gave birth to a superstition that lasted for many years.

Nat "Sweetwater" Clifton played mainly with the Knicks back in the 1950s. He obtained his moniker because he liked to mix sugar with water, inventing his own favorite drink, literally, sweet water.

Vinnie Johnson was a valuable player who often came off the bench for many successful Detroit teams. Since it took only seconds for him to enter the contest and "heat things up," he was called "Microwave."

Clarence "Foots" Walker took on that nickname from his childhood. They say his shoe size reached a whopping 11 when he was still in grade school.

Darryl Dawkins was a unique character, without question. During his NBA days, he was one of a handful of men who made it to the pro ball level straight out of high school. He was called "Double D" and "Chocolate Thunder" (years before Jason Williams, who broke in with Sacramento, was called "White Chocolate").

What also set Dawkins apart from others was he created wild and colorful nicknames for his thundering dunk shots such as: the In-Your-Face Disgrace, Go-Rilla Dunk, the Spine Chiller Supreme, Earthquaker Shaker (sometimes called Earthquake Breaker), the Hammer of Thor, Candy Slam, the Dunk You Very Much, Look Out Below Dunk, Turbo Delight, the Rim Wrecker, and, when he'd take the ball off his own rebound and run the length of the court for a dunk, he coined the phrase, Greyhound Bus as it went "coast-to-coast."

Dawkins once commented, "The fans pay your salary and you've got to excite them and bring them back." He also stated, "I wanted to make the game fun for myself. If it's work, nobody wants to do it. I made the game easy for myself."

Dunks were a big part of that fun, including what was perhaps his most famous slam ever. During a contest in Kansas City, Dawkins shattered the backboard with defender Bill Robinzine standing by helplessly while glass showered down on the court. When Dawkins destroyed another backboard three months later, the NBA devised breakaway rims in order to save money and protect players.

•

Brad Lohaus checked in at 6' 11" and a somewhat slender 230 pounds. Due to his physique and his mop of blond hair, he was called "Q-tip."

•

Bill Mlkvy had such an unusual last name, something just had to be done about it. Since he attended Temple, known as the Owls, someone pinned the names the "Owl Without a Vowel" and "The Vowelless Owl" on Mlkvy.

•

While Spencer Haywood was certainly a star, when his skills faded he decided to play ball in Europe rather than simply retire from the NBA. Because he made this move, someone gave him the derisive nickname "Driftwood."

It's hard to imagine Gail Goodrich was too keen on his nickname, "Stumpy," but by NBA standards his frame, around 6' or so, was rather stumpy. Laker teammates quickly took to calling him that name every chance they could.

Brad Daugherty joked about his nickname, "Hooch." He explained, "My wife used to call me Hooch all the time after that big ol' dog from the movie *Turner & Hooch*. She said I was such a slob, and I reminded her of that dog."

There's an old story that says one college team had two players, not related, but both named Smith, who frequently lost the ball. One wit labeled them the "Smith Brothers" because, he claimed, "They coughed up the ball so much."

7 RECORDS AND RULES

Records are an integral and fun part of basketball. The records in this chapter highlight superstar achievements and historical failures. Basketball rules have, of course, changed considerably since the game's origins. Included here are interesting facts and anecdotes regarding these changes.

When the Miami Heat came into the NBA at the start of the 1988–1989 season, they endured a miserable start. At the end of their first 17 contests, they had yet to win a single game. One writer sarcastically called the team the Miami Chill. That still stands as the record for the most straight losses to start a season.

By 1991–1992, the Heat did warm up when they managed to make the playoffs for the first time ever.

When based on the highest scoring average per game, the two best scorers in NBA history are Wilt Chamberlain and Michael Jordan. These two scoring machines averaged 30.1 ppg. However, the all-time leading scorer in the history of the NBA is *Kareem Abdul-Jabbar*. Over his stellar 20-year career, he poured in an astounding 38,387 points.

Abdul-Jabbar's average stood at 24.6, and he was still piling on the points at the ancient (by NBA standards) age of 42. And there was more to him than merely slamming down points. After his first eight years in the NBA, he had monopolized the MVP trophy, winning an astounding five of them.

Center Bob McAdoo once summed up the reality of guarding Abdul-Jabbar, "You can't let him get the position he wants or you're dead. You hope not to try and let him get down low. If he's low, you can't stop him."

Wilt Chamberlain's 1961–1962 season defies belief. For the year, he averaged over *50 ppg*. That was also the season in which he set the all-time single game record for points scored. He tossed down exactly 100 markers, an unbelievable feat!

On March 2, 1962, in Hershey, Pennsylvania, at the Fairgrounds arena, in a game witnessed by a mere 4,124 fans, the unstoppable Wilt went absolutely berserk. It was in the 169 to 147 victory by his Warriors over the New York Knicks, that Chamberlain fired shot after shot and wound up with 36 buckets made on an astounding 63 shots attempted.

It certainly didn't hurt Chamberlain's cause that the Knicks' star center, Phil Jordan, wasn't available for the game. Without him, they tried everything to halt Chamberlain, including guarding him with all five men on defense and stalling with the ball when they were on offense.

To counteract the delaying tactics, the Warriors put bench players into the game to foul the Knicks. Then, after foul shots were taken and Philadelphia got the ball back, Chamberlain's teammates continually fed him the ball.

Chamberlain, a notoriously poor free throw shooter, ended the night hitting an astounding 28 out of 32 from the charity stripe.

Chamberlain had pumped in 23 points by the end of the first period, 41 by the half, and 69 by the third quarter's buzzer. With 7:51 on the clock during the fourth stanza, his old record for the most points scored in a game toppled. His last score came with 46 seconds left to play, causing overjoyed fans to storm the court. Play was halted until order was restored.

Just prior to his death in 1999, Chamberlain spoke of how proud he was of this scoring outburst. "It has become my handle, and I've come to realize just what I did."

Remarkably, Wilt Chamberlain even led the league in assists one year. This was a feat that no center had ever done and probably never again will. Seemingly bored with scoring points at will, Chamberlain set out to prove that he could accomplish anything if he set his mind to it.

By the end of the 1967–1968 season, his 702 assists were 23 more than the total posted by the second place finisher, playmaker Lenny Wilkens. Chamberlain averaged a whopping 8.6 apg while also leading the league in rebounding, field goal percentage, and coming in third in the scoring derby as well.

The number one player in NBA history for steals is Utah legend John Stockton. Known for his good hands and his great peripheral vision, this great guard swiped the ball 3,265 times. To put that statistic in perspective, the second best steal total is more than 700 steals less than Stockton's record.

The second best in this department was hardly a slouch—it was Michael Jordan.

NBA Rules and Regulations

The NBA has strict rules and regulations on all aspects of the game. For instance, the rule book states, "The three-point field goal area has parallel lines 3' from the sidelines, extending from the baseline, and an arc of 23' 9" from the middle of the basket which intersects the parallel lines."

In other words, some of the three-pointers' distances are 22' from the hoop, but once the three-point line begins to curve away from the sidelines and up past the top of the key, the distance increases to almost 24' from the bucket.

Most experts agree that the single most important rule change in NBA history was the innovation of the 24-second shot clock.

Back in the early part of the 1950s, the league faced the problem of fan apathy due to low scoring contests. The scores were so pathetic because, without a shot clock, teams would build up an early lead in the game and then sit on the ball. That is to say, they'd dribble it and pass it endlessly in an effort to kill the clock. The team on defense would foul the stalling team in an effort to get the ball back. So fans were faced with tedious delays and a stream of players going to the foul line—boring!

Alex Sachare, who has written or contributed to several books on basketball, wrote about the advent of the shot clock, explaining that before its invention about the only strategy of the game in such situations involved good ball handlers who would "dribble until they were fouled, and the parade from one free throw line to the other would begin." Bob Cousy commented, "That was the way the game was played—get a lead and put the ball in the icebox."

Things changed when Danny Biasone, who was one of the NBA's founding fathers as owner of the Syracuse Nationals, came up with the rule stating a team had to put up a shot within 24 seconds of their having gained possession of the ball or a turnover would be called. That simple change forced teams to attack with the ball rather than merely protect it.

The league also attacked the problem of all the intentional fouling by restricting the amount of fouls a team could commit in a quarter without incurring an added penalty of the referees calling a foul a shooting foul. The rule change meant it could be a disadvantage to foul an opponent, and the game's offense suddenly spurted to life.

On November 22, 1950, prior to the 24-second clock, one game featured a *combined* 37 points, with Fort Wayne topping Minneapolis 19–18. In a 1953 contest, screeching brakes were applied to a game as 106 fouls were committed during what could have been an exciting playoff game. Alex Sachare reported that as late as 1954 a playoff game featured more foul shots taken than field goals scored (by a 75 to 34 margin).

In the first year of the shot clock, 1954–1955, the league emerged from its funk. Teams averaged in the 90s, some 13.6 points per game more than the previous season. Sachare stated that in 1954–1955 the Celtics became the first team ever to top the 100 ppg plateau for an entire year.

Just three seasons later, every single team in the league was clicking, on average, for 100+ points every night out. Biasone was quoted as saying, "Pro basketball would not have survived without a clock."

•

Long before the 24-second clock there was a rule that stated each time a team scored a basket, play was stopped and players lined up again, as they did to start each game, for another tip-off. The rule was foolish and slowed things down.

▬ ▬ ▬

Originally the basket literally was a peach basket—no net, no opening at the bottom of the basket. Therefore, every time a player scored the game was halted to retrieve the ball (at first by a janitor who sat near the "hoop" on a ladder).

In the first game ever played, under the direction of the game's creator, Dr. James A. Naismith, the two teams took to a YMCA court in Springfield, Massachusetts.

There was a grand total of one bucket scored during the entire 30-minute affair, played by using the original 13 rules of the game as drafted by Naismith.

·

The first field goal ever was scored by a man named William R. Chase.

·

Naismith, who is also the inventor of the football helmet, had no provision at first for a backboard.

·

The reason Naismith came up with the sport of basketball back in 1891 (then spelled Basket Ball as two words) was simply to have a new game that could be played inside during the winter months—to fill the void between football in the fall and baseball in the spring.

·

The reason the basket is 10 feet off the floor is because the first peach basket happened to be nailed to an overhead running track that was perched at that height.

Test Your Basketball Smarts

Let's see how familar you are with the rules and regulations of the game:

Once during a Celtics contest, Larry Bird retrieved a ball, but did so very near the baseline. Sensing he was about to fall out of bounds and seeing no open teammate, he lobbed the ball over the back of the backboard. With typical finesse, Bird's soft shot nestled into the hoop. **Question:** Is this a legal basket? **Answer:** No. Such shots are taboo, and the other team was awarded the ball.

Let's say there are two seconds left on the game clock and a player's team is winning by one point. He wants to kill the clock but he's afraid that if he passes the ball it could be intercepted and the other team could score and win on a desperation shot. Could he simply heave the ball high up near the rafters, allowing the final two ticks to evaporate off the clock? **Answer:** Yes. Unless, and it's unlikely, he throws the ball so high that it hits, say, the roof or the clock itself, this is a perfectly legal way to kill time.

With just a few ticks left on the clock Jerry West and his Lakers were down by two at the hands of the New York Knicks in Game #3 of the 1970 NBA Finals. Los Angeles inbounded the ball and West heaved the NBA's version of a Hail Mary shot. The ball flew a stunning 60 feet, landing only after it had swished through the net, forcing the game into overtime.

Fans felt the momentum had turned with his incredible shot, but the Knicks went on to win. Still, that shot remains an unforgettable playoff moment. If the shot was that far, though, why wasn't it a game-winning three-pointer?

Answer: Back in 1970 there was no such thing as a three-pointer, so the shot was breathtaking, but only worth a "deuce."

Let's say Team A has just scored a basket and the players apply pressure on Team B as they try to inbound the ball. Can the man trying to get the ball in throw it to a teammate who is also standing out of bounds by the baseline standing, say, 12 feet or so to his immediate left? Is this strategy to defeat the defensive move allowed?

Answer: The rulebook says that after a score, it is perfectly legal, as the first inbounder "may pass the ball to a teammate behind the end line; however, the five-second [limit] throw-in rule applies." In other words, Team B can use this ploy, but they still must do so in five seconds or lose the ball.

Most fans know there are numerous time limits in the NBA—24 seconds to get off a shot, 10 seconds to move the ball from the back to the front court, and so on. Many people are not aware that even the free throw shooter has a time restriction. What is it?

Answer: To quote the rulebook again: "Each free throw attempt shall be made with 10 seconds after the ball has been placed at the disposal of the free-thrower." Some refs consider rules like this to be picky, "nickel-dime" rules and give more liberty to players who tend to be deliberate at the line, especially on a key shot.

Some players had unusual mannerisms at the foul line. One player, for example, made a sort of phantom move with the ball, as if he was lining up his shot just as a golfer takes practice strokes. Another made the initial move as if to shoot, but then did a little jerky, hesitation move first. Are such habits within the rules?

Answer: While veterans with established moves such as the ones mentioned would be shocked to have referees punish them, the rulebook clearly states that the man on the line "shall not purposely fake a free throw attempt." The key is, no doubt, the word purposely. If a player did this to lure the defensive team into the lane early, anticipating a rebound and thus committing a lane violation, refs would surely act then and penalize the shooting team.

There is another rule that helps the foul shooter. It reads: "An opponent shall not disconcert the free thrower in any way, once the ball has been placed at the disposal of the shooter." Again, defensive players on the line often wait until the shooter is about to release the ball before they raise an arm or two, but they insist they're not doing this as a distraction. They claim they're merely getting in position to go for a missed shot. While some players seem to stretch this rule, it is rarely enforced.

An offensive player is hanging around under the hoop, clearly inside the three-second lane. He sees (or senses) the ref about to blow his whistle to call the violation on him. To combat the call, he quickly steps out of bounds directly under the backboard then steps back into the lane to get a new grace period of three seconds. Is this legal?

Answer: No, while a player on offense can enter, then leave the "paint" as often as he wants to get a new three-second count, he can't do this as described. The rulebook explains why: "A player shall not remain for more than three seconds in that part of his free throw lane between the endline and extended 4' (imaginary) off the court and the edge of the free throw line while the ball is in control of his team." Technically, even if a player became injured while in the paint then rolled out of bounds near the hoop where he remained immobile, he would still be called for a three-second infraction.

Imagine a player inbounding the ball from a distance of, say, 20 feet from the basket. Is he permitted to throw it towards a teammate with the intention of having him tip the ball in, but also considering the fact that if he throws it off target, there's still a slight chance the pass will go directly through the hoop for two points?

Answer: He can certainly throw the pass anywhere he wants, and, if a teammate touches the ball before it goes through the basket, that's fine. However, if his pass goes directly through the hoop, the play is illegal. That's only fair; otherwise players would simply shoot the ball from out of bounds rather than throw the ball in.

A rule that seems to confuse many amateur players is the one concerning kicking the ball. When does this rule take effect, and what is the penalty?

Answer: In the NBA, the rule clearly states that kicking or striking the ball with any part of one's leg is an infraction of the rules when "it is an intentional act. The ball accidentally striking the foot, the leg, or fist is not a violation."

The penalty for such actions is also simple: "If the violation is by the offense, the ball is awarded to the opponent at the sideline nearest the spot of the violation. If the violation is by the defense, the offensive team retains possession of the ball . . . [and] the 24-second clock is reset to 24 seconds and if the violation occurred in the back-court, a new 10-second count is awarded."

Did you know that a player is not permitted "to cause the ball to enter the basket from below"? Thus, if a ball accidentally is tipped up through the hoop and then falls back through, no score would be allowed.

And, did you know that "a player may not assist a teammate to gain height while attempting to score"? In other words, if a player thought he could get away with boosting or hoisting a teammate up high enough, for example, to dunk the ball, forget it.

A player is not permitted to "assist himself to score by using the ring or backboard to lift, hold, or raise himself." The penalty for the last two rules is the loss of the ball.

8 QUICK BIOS

Here is some interesting information on current NBA players and past greats.

Forward Carmello Anthony was the number one draft pick of the Denver Nuggets in the 2003 draft. By the end of his rookie season—which he started at the tender age of 19—he ranked #12 in the NBA in scoring at 21.0, including the sixth-most field goals made, 624, and the fifth highest total of free throws made, 408.

In college, the AP named Anthony Second-Team All-America when he was a freshman. He guided Syracuse to a 30–5 record and the school's first NCAA Championship in men's basketball. He was also picked as the Most Outstanding Player of the 2003 Final Four and East Regional and was the consensus national Freshman of the Year. After all, he had averaged 22.2 ppg, good for 16th in nation to go with his 10.0 rpg, 19th in the country.

The early success of Carmello Anthony and LeBron James was, according to the Associated Press, a huge reason that in 2003 and into 2004, basketball cards "narrowed the gap [in sales] between . . . the more traditionally popular baseball and football cards." The AP quoted an owner of a sports collectable shop as saying, "It was probably the best-selling season for cards ever."

•

LeBron James gained fame at such a young age he was on the cover of *Sports Illustrated* when he was just a junior in high school. Writers gave him not one, but two nicknames: "The Chosen One" and "King James."

Kids come out of college early, or even come to the NBA directly out of high school now more frequently than ever before now, but what James has done is still monumental. In his initial season in the NBA, he pounded home 20.9 ppg while crashing the boards for five and a half rebounds every night. He became the youngest player to score 1,000 points in NBA history, as well as the youngest to hit for 40 in a game.

When his first year ended, James still had about half a season to go before he'd turn 20 years of age. That made James the first Cavalier and the youngest player ever to be named the Rookie of the Year.

The season before the Cavs acquired him, they established a record for the smallest crowd in the history of their facility, Gund Arena. Almost exactly one year earlier, another event had set the record for the largest crowd ever at what locals call "The Gund." That event was a high school playoff contest (not even the State Finals) featuring James, who played his prep ball at Akron St. Vincent-St. Mary, not far from Cleveland.

Kevin Garnett is one of the game's more interesting players. Joining the NBA in 1995 as a mere 19-year-old, he became the first player to enter the league without playing college ball in more than 20 years, dating back to the Moses Malone era. Men such as Kobe Bryant, Tracy McGrady, Amare Stoudemire, and LeBron James followed, but Garnett was, without question, the pathfinder.

In 1996, the 6' 11" forward right out of Farragut Academy averaged only 1.8 apg, but by 2003 that total had leaped to 6.0! Likewise, as a rookie he pulled down 6.3 boards per game, but by his eighth year in the league he was hauling in 13.4 rpg.

Garnett was so versatile Memphis Grizzlies coach Hubie Brown commented, "It doesn't matter which of the four positions you play him at, he would be all-league."

Through 2003–2004, Garnett was a six-time All-Star and had been named to the All-Defensive team five times. In 2003–2004, he proved he was the complete package when he joined Larry Bird as the only men to average 20+ points, 10+ rebounds, and five or more assists per game for five straight seasons. That year, he led the league with 71 double-doubles, and was NBA MVP.

While many NBA players were conferred their state's title of "Mr. Basketball," Garnett is unusual in that he won that coveted name in *two* states. As an underclassman in South Carolina he won the honor, and the next year, after he moved to Chicago, he won it again for the state of Illinois.

•

It's tough enough to become highly skilled at one defensive position on the court, but to excel at several spots is something special. Magic Johnson weighed 220 pounds and stood 6' 9"—considered to be a fine height for a forward. However, his passing and ball handling skills were top notch and he played point guard like few other men could.

When Game #6 of the NBA Finals of 1980 rolled around, Lakers' starting center Kareem Abdul-Jabbar was nursing an injured ankle and didn't make the trip to Philadelphia. Johnson, then only 20 years of age, had to step in to handle the all-important task of guarding Darryl Dawkins, who checked in at 6' 11" and 252 pounds.

Johnson racked up 42 points, dished the ball off 15 times, and collected seven rebounds. During the course of the game, Johnson wound up playing every position on the court. He later joked that he had played "center, a little forward, some guard. I tried to think up a name for it, but the best I could come up with was CFG-Rover."

Johnson went on to win the Finals MVP trophy for his showing, and would win that award two more times. He also won the regular season MVP award on three occasions and helped lead his Lakers to the NBA championship five times.

Jason Kidd was the second overall pick in the 1994 draft behind only Glenn Robinson. When Kidd broke in with the Dallas Mavericks, he asked for jersey number 32 to symbolize his goal in the game, racking up "triple-doubles."

Kidd has many talents, but none more glittering than his playmaking skills. From 1998 through 2003, his 4,234 assists ranked number one in the NBA. The tough defender also rebounds well for a guard, averaging over 6.0 per game for his career.

Former Knicks guard Walt Frazier called Kidd "faster than Magic [Johnson]." Isiah Thomas chipped in, "Kidd is the closest thing to Magic in this league." That is the ultimate compliment to Kidd, as his basketball role models were John Stockton and Johnson.

Even when Larry Bird was new to the NBA, it was clear that he was special. Celtics General Manager Red Auerbach attested, "He's a big [Bob] Cousy. I never thought I'd compare anyone with Cousy. But Larry Bird has those great hands and great vision. He has a great concept of the game, a great feeling for what's going on between the foul lines. He's got patience, he's strong, and he's unselfish."

The great forward from French Lick, Indiana (his actual birthplace was West Baden, Indiana) also was a 12-time All-Star over his 13-year career. He was the first player not to play the center position who earned three straight MVP trophies. Most experts feel he would be one of the two forwards if they had to pick an all-time NBA team.

Bird could do it all—he even compiled 5,695 assists even though he was never a point guard. So, call him a point forward, and a great one at that.

Bill Walton became quite accustomed to winning on basketball courts at every level of play. In high school, he won consecutive state titles and ran up a string of 49 games won in a row. He also established a standard for shooting excellence over the course of a season. During the 1969–1970 season, he fired the ball up 490 times and sank 384 of those shots, good for a record .783 field goal percentage.

The UCLA team Walton was on not only won the NCAA championship in 1972 and 1973, it also chalked up an unbelievable 88 consecutive wins! Walton's performance in the 1973 championship game is, some say, the greatest single performance in Final Four play ever. He shot the ball 22 times, making every shot but one. In all, he registered 44 points and gathered 13 rebounds to top Memphis State.

Walton's finest hour in NBA play was probably his third year in the league. As a Portland Trailblazer, the 6' 11" center led all players in rebounds and blocked shots. He then guided his team to a championship over the Philadelphia 76'ers, even though Portland was down two games to none at one point.

If it weren't for so many nagging injuries, who knows what kind of numbers Walton could have amassed in the NBA. Sadly, over his four-year stint in Portland, Walton played in 209 games but sat out 201 contests. Then it got worse; over the next two seasons he played in just 14 and 33 games.

Still, Walton was an integral part of two teams who captured NBA titles. The Associated Press described Walton's skills as such: "[He] ripped rebounds off the rim, fired laser-like outlet passes, swatted away opponents' shots, and hit curling teammates with over-the-shoulder no-look passes."

Walton was voted into the Hall of Fame as a member of its Class of '93 and was even named to the 50 Greatest Players in NBA History—even though he played in a grand total of only 468 pro contests.

Oscar Robertson's legendary status goes back to college, where, playing for the University of Cincinnati, he was a three-time scoring champ and the all-time leading playmaker based on total assists for many a year. He became the first sophomore ever to lead the nation in scoring, doing so in 1957–1958 at 35.1 ppg.

It would have been impossible for Robertson to lead the country in scoring as a freshman. At that time, a rule prohibited freshmen from playing on the "varsity" level.

In his rookie season in the NBA, Oscar Robertson, nearly averaged double figures in three statistical departments. At 6'5", Robertson was considered tall for a guard back in the 1960s, giving him an edge as he easily shot over defenders.

The next year "The Big O" averaged triple-doubles for the entire season. No player had ever accomplished this feat before Robertson, and experts doubt if anyone else ever will. Robertson's exact totals were an awesome 30.8 ppg, 12.5 rpg (a great total for a guard), and 11.4 apg.

Through 2004, Robertson's career total of 181 "triple-doubles" remained by far the best in NBA annals. The nearest to him is Magic Johnson with 138, followed by Wilt Chamberlain's 78, and Larry Bird, who recorded 59. Robertson was named to the All-NBA First Team nine consecutive seasons.

John Stockton's name goes hand-in-hand with Oscar Robertson in that he eventually emerged as the all-time leader for total assists. Stockton wasn't limited to merely passing the ball, however, as he was a sharpshooter, a pickpocket on defense (setting the record for career steals), and he could run the pick-and-roll play (mainly with Karl Malone) perhaps better than any ballplayer ever.

Stockton was so durable he became one of only seven men to last in the league until the age of 42. In addition, the Utah star played in every single one of his team's games for 17 seasons.

Jerry West, a rugged 6' 2" guard, was one of the all-time greats. According to the NBA website, West grew up in West Virginia and, without much money, "his only outlet was a basketball hoop nailed to a storage shed outside a neighbor's house. The dirt-covered court became his domain. In the rainy spring he dribbled in mud. When it snowed West played wearing gloves. He practiced shooting until his fingers bled." West starred in his home state in both high school and at West Virginia University. Throughout his basketball career, he would prove to be an intense and resilient ballplayer, sustaining a broken nose on nine or more occasions.

West entered the NBA as a splinter-thin kid who signed for a measly bonus of $1,500 plus a salary of $15,000. A great jump shooter, he played 14 years in the league and was an All-Star in each of those seasons. In four of those campaigns, he averaged 30 or more points. He lit up the scoreboards for a lifetime average of 27 ppg. The ultimate pressure player, he did even better in post-season play, at 29.1 ppg. It's hard to say what his career average would have been if he played when the three-pointer was in effect.

West played tough "D" as well. He was named to the NBA All-Defensive First Team four times.

West helped his Lakers make it to the NBA Finals nine times. Later he not only coached the Lakers for three seasons, he also was a part of their front office for over 20 years. His short tenure as a coach was due, what else, to getting fired. However, in his case there was a twist to the scenario—the perfectionist West fired himself!

The official NBA logo, which features the outline of a player dribbling a ball, was patterned after West.

In his second season, and first as a starter, Kevin Johnson, blessed with an explosive first step, blossomed as a star. He guided the Phoenix Suns to an awe-inspiring one-season improvement over the previous year, up some 27 victories.

In that season, Johnson became just the fifth player ever to top 20 ppg while also handing out 10 or more apg. The other elite players to do that were Oscar Robertson, Nate Archibald, Magic Johnson, and Isiah Thomas. For all his toil and terrific stats, he easily won the Most Improved Player of the Year Award.

K.J., as he was called, was so athletic he was drafted by the Oakland A's as a shortstop. When he didn't hit well, it allowed him to, as he put it, "get baseball out of my system." Things hadn't always been so easy for him—his father died when he K.J. was only three and he was brought up in the ghetto of Sacramento by his mother's parents.

As an adult, Johnson gave back to the community, most notably by forming the St. HOPE Academy. He built "a place where young people could come for unconditional love, support and nurturing, a place where the focus would be on self-esteem and character. When one commits himself from the heart, nothing is difficult." A St. HOPE executive said with a smile, "When he's with the kids, he's like a big kid himself."

Shaquille Rashaun O'Neal's first and middle names, when translated from Arabic, mean "Little Warrior." When O'Neal signed with the Lakers in 1996, it seemed just a matter of time before he'd lead them to an NBA title. Sure enough, in 1999–2000 he earned an MVP trophy and guided his team to the championship. They went on to "three-peat," with O'Neal winning the Finals MVP award in all three of those magnificent seasons.

Joe Fulks dazzled fans with his scoring fireworks. The official website of basketball's Hall of Fame states that Fulks "was considered modern pro basketball's first scoring sensation, revolutionizing shooting and scoring by first using a two-handed shot and then gradually switching to the one-handed method."

Fulks began his college career at Murray State in Kentucky (1941–1943) shooting the ball in the style of the times, using a two-hand set shot. That fashion, which looks primitive by today's standards, featured the shooters' two hands releasing the ball from about the level of his nose while the player was basically flatfooted.

Fulks changed all that when he employed the one-hand jumper we know today. Much harder to block, this shot became a lethal weapon in his, and shortly thereafter in others', hands (actually, make that "hand," singular).

One publication was so taken with Fulk's discovery and his scoring outbursts, they labeled him the "Babe Ruth of basketball."

Veteran guard Sam Cassell had nothing but kind words for Tracy McGrady when he observed: "People talk about Kobe [Bryant], [Allen] Iverson, and the other guys, but to me, Tracy is the best player in the league behind Shaq [O'Neal]. More than anyone else, he does it all."

McGrady's 26.8 ppg in 2000–2001 stood as the fourth best scoring average in NBA history for a player who began a season at the age of 21 or younger. The only players to outscore him were Oscar Robertson at 30.5 ppg way back in 1961, O'Neal at 29.3 in 1994, and Michael Jordan who averaged 28.2 in 1985. However, no man had ever scored more when based on the highest average for a player who had turned 21 by the end of a season.

By the next season, McGrady, a youngster who came to the league straight out of Mount Zion Christian Academy, was named to the All-Star squad.

In the 2001–2002 and 2002–2003 seasons, McGrady was named to the All-NBA First Team. In 2002–2003, McGrady finished as the NBA's leading scorer (32.1 ppg.), and averaged 1.65 spg and 5.5 apg. He was also named a starter for the East at the 2004 NBA All-Star Game.

•

Even though the 6' 9" Elvin Hayes went on to become an all-time NBA great, many fans still remember him for a tremendous collegiate performance. As a member of the Houston Cougars, he had to take on Lew Alcindor, then in his junior year, and the UCLA Bruins when they came to town for a January 20, 1969 showdown. It was a matchup between the number one and number two teams in the nation. The highly touted Alcindor had steered his Bruins to an undefeated streak that had run to 47 games!

The event was too big for a mere college gym so, in front of a national television audience, a rare occurrence back then, the game was held in the Astrodome. The dream game packed some 52,693 fans into the dome, a staggering total for a college game. Some experts called this event "the game that put college basketball on the map."

In the end, Houston pulled off a fantastic upset to snap the Bruins string of wins. Not at all surprisingly, Hayes was the big gun with 39 points (four-tenths of a point over what would be his scoring average in that, his senior year) to go along with his 15 rebounds.

By the end of Hayes' professional career, no man had played more minutes in the history of the NBA (over 16 seasons he missed a mere nine games), and only two men had scored more points than he had. His 21 ppg average was third best in NBA history. He pulled down an average per game of 12.5 rebounds, again third best in history at the time of his retirement. Hayes was a twelve-time NBA All-Star during the period 1969–1980.

The Hall of Fame was Hayes' next destination, as he was inducted there in 1989.

Wilt Chamberlain, probably the most dominating player to ever lace sneakers, began his magical ways back on the playgrounds and in the gyms of Philadelphia. From there it was on to Kansas, where his reputation grew to be as large as his 7' 1" frame and 270-plus lbs.

The four-time NBA MVP was selected to 13 All-Star games. Chamberlain led the NBA in scoring seven consecutive years (1959–65), rebounding 11 times, and in 1968 led the league in assists.

By the time his illustrious career was over, Chamberlain owned more records than any player.

One of the most interesting college players from the 2004–2005 season was Andrew Bogut, a highly touted seven-footer. He attracted notice when he entered the United States in 2001 as a player for the Australian Institute of Sport (AIS). He toured the country while playing exhibition contests against college teams.

Later Bogut gained more recognition at the University of Utah starting as a freshman when he averaged 12.5 ppg to go with his 9.9 rpg. By the end of the 2004–2005 NCAA season, experts called him the best player in the nation and felt that a long career in the world of the NBA was inevitable.

It sure didn't take Jason "Pooh" Richardson, the fifth overall draft pick in 2001, long to show the NBA that he was for real. He was a member of the 2002 NBA All-Rookie First Team (he finished third in Rookie of the Year voting), and by the end of the 2003–2004 season he already stood fourth on the Warriors all-time three-point field goal list, with 282.

Richardson won the 2002 and 2003 Slam Dunk Contests to join Michael Jordan, the winner in 1997 and 1998, as the only players to win the contest in back-to-back years. In fact, in 2002 he became the first player to win both the MVP of the Rookie Challenge and the Slam Dunk Contest.

The man known as "J-Rich" was, believe it or not, great on the ice as well as the court, playing hockey until he was in eighth grade and his feet outgrew his ice skates. Perhaps he could have excelled in prizefighting or flying, too, with a wingspan of nearly seven feet.

Richardson was named Michigan's Mr. Basketball in 1998–99 after leading his team to a berth in Michigan's Class A title game. He was quickly noticed by the entire nation, naturally, and was selected as a McDonald's All-American after averaging 25.3 points and 12.8 rebounds as a senior.

•

Nate Thurmond once said of Brad Daugherty, "He's one of the three or four best centers in the league. He does it all: he's an excellent passer; he's not a great shot blocker, but he plugs up the middle."

Thurmond added that on a winning team, "You start with a center, and he's right there. He's right up there with [Patrick] Ewing and [Hakeem] Olajuwon."

Daugherty, the grandson of a full-blooded Cherokee, loves to hunt and fish and does almost any activity involving the outdoors. He even joked that he is, at 7' tall, the world's tallest water skier. "I look like a big pole coming across the water," he chuckled.

Dave Robinson was not like most NBA stars in that he didn't excel in his youth. He even quit his ninth-grade team and didn't play again until he reached 6' 7" in his senior year. Even then, he was the backup center on the team.

The San Antonio Spurs drafted Robinson in 1987, even though they realized he could not suit up with them until he had served a two-year commitment, wearing a quite different uniform, for the U.S. Navy. At the Naval Academy, David Robinson underwent a stunning growth spurt, growing six inches to his full adult height of 7' 1".

The wait paid off as Robinson led the San Antonio Spurs on the greatest one-year turnabout in NBA history. He took them from a miserable 21–61 slate to the promised lands of the playoffs, sporting a team record 56 victories.

Robinson's rookie season was so laudatory that he swept Rookie of the Month honors for six straight months over the season and unanimously won the Rookie of the Year Award.

Veteran coach Don Nelson evaluated Robinson early on, saying, "He has everything—strength, quickness, size, and speed. He has all he's going to need."

As a member of the Kentucky Wildcats, and later in professional stints with Boston (then Dallas and Atlanta), Antoine Walker put up some sensational numbers. As a freshman on the Wildcats, Walker was named MVP of his conference's tournament. In his sophomore year, he led the 1996 NCAA champion Wildcats in rebounding and minutes, while coming in second on the team in scoring (15.2 ppg), assists, and steals.

As for his pro stats, start with 1996–1997 when this high-flying forward scored the second-most points (1,435) of any rookie in Celtics history, trailing only Larry Bird's 1,745. The next year, Walker topped the Celtics in points at 22.4 ppg (good for the fifth best in the NBA), rebounds (10.2 rpg, seventh best), and double-doubles (47, second in the league).

Throughout his NBA career, Antoine has been in the top ten in points scored, minutes played, 3-point field goals, triple doubles, and defensive rebounds.

The hardworking, powerful Elton Brand took off big in the NBA. He was named the co-winner of the 1999–2000 Schick Rookie of the Year Award, along with Steve Francis.

Not too long after that, he made his first career All-Star appearance—on the 2002 Western Conference All-Star Team, the year he ranked first in the league in total offensive rebounds with 396.

In college, Brand was an absolute superstar for the Duke Blue Devils. In his sophomore season, he corralled almost as many awards as his team had victories. After leading Duke in scoring (17.7 ppg), rebounding (9.8 rpg), and blocked shots (86), Brand was the consensus National Player of the Year and a unanimous First Team All-American selection by the Associated Press. He was also the 1999 Atlantic Coast Conference Player of the Year and USA Basketball's Man of the Year.

Brand's career field-goal percentage mark of .621 was the highest ever for players with at least 300 shots sunk, and he ranked fifth for career blocked shots at Duke.

Then Brand disappointed and saddened Duke fans by becoming their first player ever to announce he would leave the school early for the NBA. Still, he made those same fans proud when he became the first Blue Devil ever to be picked with the top choice in the NBA Draft when Chicago took him at number one in 1999.

•

The master of the moves in the paint area, Kevin McHale began his NBA career in 1980. Thirteen years later, as a Boston Celtic, he had earned three NBA championship rings and had drilled in thousands of points. He, fellow forward Larry Bird, and center Robert Parish formed what is probably the greatest frontcourt in the history of the game.

McHale is famous for his intelligence (moving to the front office after he was done playing the game), as well as for his great moves such as his head fakes and his "up and under" fakes.

McHale was a member of either the first or second team on the All-NBA Defensive Team six times, blocking many a shot with his long arms, which seemingly rivaled those of Spiderman's foe, Doctor Octopus.

In 6' 10" Chris Webber, one sees a player who does many things well. In 1993-1994, for example, he became the first NBA rookie to total more than 1,000 points, 500 rebounds, 250 assists, 150 blocks, and 75 steals, earning him the Schick NBA Rookie of the Year Award.

Webber made his first All-Star appearance in 1997, and in 2001, his first All-Star Game *start*. Later that season he was a member of the All-NBA First Team, thanks largely to his 27.1 ppg and 11.1 rpg. He even finished fourth in the MVP voting for the 2000–2001 season. In the NBA official web site, he was described as "a rare blend of strength, speed, size and skill."

In his collegiate days, Webber spent two seasons at the University of Michigan. There he was the key member of a class of five players that started as freshmen and earned the nickname the "Fab Five." And what a talented bunch of players they were, rounded out by Juwan Howard, Jalen Rose, Jimmy King, and Ray Jackson. Despite their youth and inexperience, that squad rolled on until they were knocked off by Duke in the 1992 NCAA title game.

Webber was a First Team All-America selection and a finalist for the Wooden and Naismith Awards as a sophomore, leading the Wolverines to the NCAA Championship Game in both of his collegiate seasons. He was the leading rebounder and second-leading scorer in the 1993 NCAA Tournament, but his big mistake as time was winding down at the end of the championship game against the University of North Carolina is a brand he will forever wear.

Michigan was trailing by only two points with 11 seconds left when Webber signaled for a timeout. However, what he forgot was his Wolverines had already used all of their timeouts, so they were assessed a technical foul. The Tar Heels went on to win the game, 77–71, aided by his terrible error.

Earl "The Pearl" Monroe got his nickname in college at Winston-Salem. His first four games produced 33-, 68-, 58-, and 59-point bursts, prompting a newspaper writer to state, "These are Earl's pearls."

The same could have been said of his moves. Phil Jackson commented, "His style of play evokes an attitude of freedom. He dips, he darts, you don't know what he'll do next."

Another player muttered in awe, "He's revolutionized the guard position with those spin moves and turning and twisting. Before that started, it was almost forbidden to turn your back to the basket so you couldn't see the whole floor. He started something no one else could do."

Monroe was a four-time NBA All-Star. He played 926 career games, scored 17,454 total points (18.8 ppg) and dished out 3,594 assists. He helped the New York Knicks win the 1973 NBA championship.

Scottie Pippen was a player who, according to wire services, "played the sidekick to basketball's greatest star [Michael Jordan], creating a partnership the Chicago Bulls parlayed into an NBA dynasty with six titles in the 1990s."

When Pippen arrived on the Bulls scene, Jordan was already a big name, but it still took the two men and a cast of supporting characters four seasons to win their first crown. That was the beginning of the first of two "three-peat" runs of championships. The 1996 Chicago Bulls team won an NBA record 72 games in a season.

Pippen, who played until he reached 40 years of age, survived 17 years in the league. He is a member of the best 50 players of all-time NBA play as selected in 1996.

Nobody worked harder than Adrian Dantley did under the hoop, crashing the boards for many an offensive rebound and drawing a plethora of fouls. He was especially adept at going to the free throw line—one year he went to the line 946 times.

Since Dantley made his living down low, he was able to record a .540 field-goal percentage, one of the highest ever recorded by an NBA non-center. He was also a fine outside shot, and possessed an explosive first step.

Julius Erving recognized assets that made Dantley so tough. "[He] is strong and moves well," Erving began. "I have a harder time with guys who are shorter than me but who have a lot of quickness. . . He's strong and he's pretty heavy and he's just 6' 5". But he moves his legs well and plays position defense. Unless you go to a post-up game, he can neutralize you."

In all, the Notre Dame great, who started his career by winning Rookie of the Year honors, played in 955 NBA contests and averaged 24.3 ppg, ninth on the NBA career scoring list at the time of his retirement. His finest years ran from 1980–1981 through 1983–1984 with the Utah Jazz, when he averaged 30 or more points per contest each season. Both years he led the NBA in scoring.

Since scoring 20,000 points is considered to be a mark of excellence, label Dantley outstanding—he drained 23,177 points over his glorious career.

Long before he became a teammate of Magic Johnson, James Worthy was labeled "another Earvin Johnson" by a college coach. That's how good Worthy was even in high school.

Another coach looked at Worthy, who had already reached his adult height (6' 9") when he was in his junior year at Ashbrook High in Gastonia, North Carolina, and said, "He could play point guard at a lot of colleges right now."

Worthy went on to star at the University of North Carolina, with 1982 being his finest hour. It was then that he, as a junior, was on *The Sporting News All-America* first team, was named NCAA Division I Tournament Most Outstanding Player, and guided his Tar Heels to the national championship.

Worthy left UNC after that, snatched up by the Lakers as the first pick overall in the 1982 draft. He hooked up with Magic Johnson, and was named to the All-Rookie team.

Worthy and Johnson were teammates for nine wonderful seasons, including three years in which they won it all—in 1985, 1987, and 1988. The final of those three titles featured Worthy winning the MVP Award in the NBA Finals.

In November of 1994 he announced his retirement, having played in seven All-Star games and nine playoffs over his 12 seasons. He was destined to become a member of the NBA's 50th Anniversary All-Time Team two years later.

9 MEMORABLE PLAYS AND FEATS

NBA history is rich with unusual plays, memorable contests, awe-inspiring individual feats, and some legendary low moments. Here is a sampling.

On December 13, 1983, an NBA contest involving a scoring explosion took place that may never be forgotten. Denver hosted Detroit in a game that ran into triple overtime. When the final buzzer gave an exhausted blare, the final score read Detroit 186 and Denver 184— good for a record 370 combined tallies, some 33 points higher than the old mark.

Kelly Tripucka, who scored 35, commented on the three hour and 11 minute game, "After this game both teams deserve a week off. It seems like we played three games. You couldn't write a book with a better script."

Detroit coach Chuck Daly mused, "They usually say the first team to 100 will win the game, but in this one that happened in the middle of the third quarter." On that same day, Chicago beat Milwaukee in a contest which featured a total of only 184 points, less than half of what Detroit and Denver rained down.

In January of 1999, a strange play occurred during a game between the University of Cincinnati and UNC Charlotte. With 17.5 seconds left, a Charlotte player missed a foul shot in a one-on-one situation. Cincinnati grabbed the rebound off the miss and Melvin Levett soon hit a three-pointer to put his Bearcats on top. However, the ref, perhaps thinking the teams were in a foul situation calling for two shots, blew the ball dead and the three-point shot didn't count.

Later, upon reviewing the play, the league ruled that while the ref was unquestionably wrong, the loss would not be overturned and UNC Charlotte's 62–60 win stayed on the books. The official was publicly criticized, but the ruling (and the ref's mistake) cost Cincinnati a victory.

Wilt Chamberlain was a dominating seven-footer who starred for Philadelphia, San Francisco, and Los Angeles from 1959 to 1973.

Early in his career, his team devised a trick play to take advantage of his size. When a teammate was inbounding the ball near their basket, he would lob the ball over the backboard. Chamberlain would simply take off, grab the pass, and stuff it into the hoop. The play was unstoppable. However, it didn't take too long until the league came up with a rule to outlaw this scheme.

Although Wilt Chamberlain was a splendid scorer, he had a mental block when it came to shooting free throws. He tried just about every style and trick in the book, including throwing the ball underhand, "granny style."

Nothing worked, until he decided to use his leaping ability to his advantage. Chamberlain would start his foul shot by backing up way behind the free throw line. Then he would blast off, running up to the line, and soaring towards the hoop. At the height of his jump, by then quite near the rim, he would toss the ball at the easy target.

Well, as is the case with many such gimmicks, once the rulesmakers thought the trick over, they decided to make it illegal. Now a player must stay in the semi-circle above the free throw line and not cross that line before releasing the ball.

One of the most unbelievable sights ever witnessed on a basketball court happened as part of an exhibition, not in a "real game." As part of the celebrations for the 1976 ABA All-Star Weekend in Denver, the league decided to host a dunk contest featuring their greatest and flashiest players.

The combatants were the dazzling Julius Erving, the towering Artis Gilmore, the acrobatic George Gervin, the skywalking David Thompson, and the high-scoring Larry Kenon.

According to the *Official NBA Encyclopedia*, Thompson stirred the crowd with "the first recorded 360-degree dunk." Erving's first dunk was impressive—he stood under the bucket and slammed home *two balls during one jump*. His second dunk, though, was monumental, truly an astounding event.

Erving began by strolling to the foul line; then he "started measuring his steps back to the other end of the court. People guessed what was coming and they were frenzied." He didn't disappoint—Dr. J raced towards the hoop, picking up his pace at mid-court. When he reached the free throw stripe, he floated high, defying gravity, coming down only to slam the ball through the hoop. The crowd erupted, as history had just been made.

While one version of the dunk slightly diminishes his accomplishment, the truth should be told. That account states that Erving did not take off from behind the line, but began his mighty jump from about two inches *inside* the line. Still, it was a remarkable performance for the doctor.

It took a Herculean effort by a big-time shooter to win the scoring title on the final day of the 1977–1978 season. On that occasion, two players staged a wild shootout tabbed "the most remarkable finish in NBA history" by one writer.

The battle was for the NBA scoring title. The contestants were San Antonio's George Gervin, a 6' 7" guard who would win four scoring crowns over a five-year span, and Denver's David Thompson, a four-time All-Star who is considered by many to be the greatest college player ever. Both men came to the NBA when the old ABA folded.

When the season finales of the two stars began back on April 9, 1978, Gervin was averaging 26.7 ppg to Thompson's 26.6. Thompson exploded from the opening whistle. He sank his first eight shots, had the next one rejected, then hit on his next 12, sizzling for 53 first half points.

Gervin knew he needed 58 points to win the scoring crown and, amazingly, he topped Thompson with relative ease. In the second quarter he drilled 33 points. Just a minute and a half into the third quarter Gervin had already pumped in 59 points. So, in one day, Chamberlain's

16-year old record for the most points tallied in a quarter, 31, tumbled not once, but *twice*.

The two scorers combined for a mind-boggling 136 points. Thompson's total of 73 points was the third highest for a single game in the history of the NBA. Gervin wound up with 63, and ended up winning the only scoring title ever to be carried out mathematically to two decimal points. Gervin topped Thompson by a 27.22 to 27.15 margin, a gap of just *seven hundredths of a point*!

•

Back on April 18th of 1962, the Lakers experienced a heartbreaking defeat, losing to the Boston Celtics. What made it so hard to take was the facts that: it was a loss in the NBA Finals, and was during a game that went a remarkable *seven* overtime sessions!

At the end of regulation play, Laker Frank Selvy missed a wide open, short jump shot. A miss of a mere inch or so cost Los Angeles the title; they fought on in seemingly endless overtime periods, but ultimately lost, 110–107.

In 1954, Frank Selvy scored a spectacular 100 points in a single game while playing for Furman against Newberry College. He sank his last bucket, to reach 100 points on the nose, when he fired up a desperation shot at the buzzer from a spot near half court. That showing helped him on his way to establishing an NCAA record of 2,538 career points.

In women's play, Cheryl Miller, sister of NBA's Reggie Miller, once pounded down an incredible 105 points during a 1982 high school game while playing for her Riverside, California team. However, more amazingly, while Lisa Leslie's (of the Los Angeles Sparks) Morningside High school team of Inglewood, California, was in the midst of drilling South Torrance High School, Leslie rattled off 101 (of her team's 102 points) by the end of the first half! There's no telling how many points she would have wound up with because the opposing coach, in sheer disgust at what he was seeing, pulled his team off the court at the half. His team had managed to score a mere 24 markers.

Clarence "Bevo" Francis played for a small school named Rio Grande. In 1953, his team went 39–0, including a big win in which Francis scored an astronomical 116 points. Because he achieved this against a junior college (Ashland), a national coaches association stripped him of this record.

The next year against a school with a four-year program, Francis again broke the century mark for points—his 113 markers still stands as a single game record.

Only Frank Selvy and Francis, who never played in the NBA, ever managed to hit the 100-point plateau in a game at the collegiate level, and they did so within 11 days of each other (with Selvy following Francis's act).

One memorable Celtics win came in June of 1976 when they topped the Phoenix Suns by a 128–126 score in three overtimes. To this day, many label that Game #5 in the Finals as the greatest game in the annals of the NBA.

At the end of the first overtime, the Celtics called for a timeout even though they had none left. The rules state that the penalty for doing that is a technical foul. Had the refs called the foul, the Suns could've won the game if they connected on a foul shot. However, the refs ignored the Celtics' signal for a timeout and the game rambled on.

As the second overtime session ended, the Celtics had just scored to take a one-point lead when the buzzer blew. The referees ruled that the clock was wrong and put one second back on the board. The Suns then intentionally called for a timeout that they didn't have coming. This time the refs made the call and the Celtics sank a free throw to take a two-point lead.

However, the Suns got possession of the ball, presented with the ball at mid-court, and not at the far baseline as they would have if they hadn't strategically called for the "extra" timeout. Garfield Heard swished a desperation shot with a microsecond left on the clock, forcing the game into a third overtime.

Finally, Boston inched ahead, won by a slim 128 to 126 margin, and went on to take the NBA title in Game #6, just two days after the marathon contest.

Larry Bird was one of the smartest basketball players ever. On May 26, 1987, in front of a friendly Celtics crowd at the Boston Gardens, Bird showed his fans yet another example of his court savvy.

It was Game #5 of the Eastern Conference Finals. By the final seconds of the game, the Detroit Pistons held a slim edge, 107–106. Since they had possession of the ball, all they had to do was inbound the ball and kill the clock. That's when Bird took over. He somehow sensed where Isiah Thomas was going to throw the ball to inbound it. Cutting in front of Piston big man Bill Laimbeer, Bird swiped the ball. Then he found teammate Dennis Johnson, fired the ball to him, and the Celtics scored the winning bucket with one tick left on the scoreboard.

Later Bird revealed to the media his thought process after he stole the ball. Bird explained that he had been keeping track of how many seconds were left in the game by counting the time down in his head. He knew his best option was the pass, and he was aware that he had enough time to get the ball to Johnson. From there, it was on to the championship in seven games for Boston.

Bill Sharman's days in the NBA began in the dark ages of 1948 with the old Washington Capitals franchise. After one season, the franchise disbanded, and he eventually became a player for the Boston Celtics where, teamed with Bob Cousy in the backcourt, they won four championships and five division titles.

Sharman once told *Basketball Digest* that despite his showing in the 1955 All-Star game when he sank 15 points in just 18 minutes to win the MVP trophy, he had an even greater NBA moment.

It took place when he was coaching the 1971–1972 Lakers, the team that streaked to a record 33 consecutive wins, never losing from the opening week of November in 1971 until the first week in January of the following year. His team also rolled to a record 69 wins while dropping only 13 decisions (a mark later broken by Michael Jordan's Bulls). Interestingly, Sharman's selection for the game he'd never forget was not the one in which the Lakers nailed the title, but an earlier playoff game.

Coming off an embarrassing loss to Kareem Abdul-Jabbar's Milwaukee Bucks in the first game of the semi-finals, Sharman believed the next game was a make or break contest. By halftime his players, led by Jerry West, Gail Goodrich, and Jim McMillian, had scored as many points, 72, as they had in the entire first game defeat.

As the game wound down, L.A. had a one-point lead, but Abdul-Jabbar grabbed the ball from West and had an open court ahead of him. Just when it looked as if he'd break away for the game-winning shot, at the moment he turned to dribble up court, the ball made contact with a referee's leg and ricocheted off to West, who held it until the buzzer ended the wild game.

Sharman said such an oddity "happens about once in 10,000 plays or more," but that wonderful break, he felt, was highly instrumental in the Lakers' march to the title that year.

No matter what else New York Knicks center Willis Reed achieved as an NBA player—and he accomplished quite a lot—he is best remembered for a short jog he took from the locker room out onto the court. It was the night of the deciding game of the 1970 Finals, May 8th, and, due to a torn thigh muscle, Reed was expected to sit the game out against the Los Angeles Lakers (as he had in Game #6 when opposing center Wilt Chamberlain went berserk, hitting for 45 points).

The home crowd noticed Reed had not even warmed up at Madison Square Garden, so pessimism set in. However, when Reed finally hobbled into view, the crowd erupted. Teammate Bill Bradley remembered, "When Willis came out onto the court, it was like the place exploded. Chills were going up and down everyone's spines." Minutes later when Reed, who couldn't even jump center for the opening tip-off, scored the first point of the game against the Lakers, fans felt a victory was sealed.

Even though Reed, noticeably limping, would only score one more bucket all night long, the Knicks did win their first NBA championship that night, 113–99, running high on emotion as well as on talent.

•

On May 10, 1993, Julius "Dr. J" Erving paid a very special visit to Springfield, Massachusetts. The occasion was his induction into the Hall of Fame. Writer Fran Blinebury stated that the good doctor "did for basketball what the Wright Brothers did for passenger travel—he took it airborne."

Counting his playing days in both the ABA and the NBA Erving scored more pro points than all but three men, all-time greats Abdul-Jabbar, Chamberlain, and Karl Malone. In 1974 and 1976, he led the Nets to the ABA championship. In 1983, Erving led the Philadelphia 76'ers to the NBA championship.

"It's a very special honor," Erving beamed the day of his entrance into the Hall of Fame.

He added he didn't expect to be a standout until he grew nearly four inches during his college days. "That helped me out a lot. It prohibited me from ever taking anything for granted. It made me have realistic expectations, focus on my studies first, and have a more balanced approach to life."

Few players had a following as wide and as loyal as Erving had, helping to make his induction a memorable moment in NBA history.

The place was Munich, Germany, and the time setting was the 1972 Olympics. The shameful moment was a pathetic display of poor sportsmanship and outright cheating—it was the year the United States had a gold medal plucked from its grasp.

Since basketball had been introduced to the Olympics in 1936, the USA had rolled like a juggernaut, collecting seven consecutive gold medals while racking up a fantastic 63–0 record. It would not just win, it would win big. Even in championship games, the USA team won by an average of about 23 points. The '72 squad—which featured such future NBA stars as Bobby Jones, Doug Collins, and Tom McMillen—was expected to continue the dynasty.

When the USA squared off against the team from the USSR for the gold, it was the fourth such meeting of these intense rivals. This time, the USA struggled and was losing at the half by five and even trailed by as many as 10 in the second half. Still, the USA did take its first lead at 50–49, just moments before the chaos was unleashed.

With mere seconds to play the Soviet team tossed an inbound pass, which was deflected by the defense as time lapsed. USA had won the gold again! But wait. The referees ruled there should still be one second on the clock, so the USSR inbounded once more. The pass fell short of its target and time again expired. But wait! An official who technically didn't even have the power to make a call disallowed the play, saying there should have been three seconds on the clock—he allowed yet another play to be run.

Later a *New York Times* writer suggested, "It began to look as if the officials would give the Russians the extra three seconds for as long as it took them to shoot the winning field goal." And that's just about what happened. They heaved a full-court throw to Aleksander Belov who, along with two defenders, "went up for the ball, but the

Americans were knocked off by Belov who suddenly found himself with an incredibly easy lay-up."

The lay-up was so easy because the biased refs ignored three Soviet infractions: 1) Belov's "clear out" of the defenders was akin to a mugging; 2) The inbounding passer stepped on the baseline while firing the key pass; 3) Belov had illegally set himself up in the three-seconds lane for "as many as five seconds."

While the USA did protest the farce, the outcome seemed clear. So, before a five-man jury reached their verdict to let the win stand, the stunned and disgusted Americans held their own meeting and voted to refuse the silver medal for a second-place finish. What began as a showcase for superb athletes from 124 nations ended as a cruel and ridiculous joke.

As a final note, Belov was possibly good enough to play in the NBA. As a matter of fact, he was drafted by the New Orleans Jazz in the 10th round in 1975 even though Soviet policy would not allow him to sign with them.

Johnny Most was the Celtics announcer for decades. The gravely voiced local legend normally painted a great play-by-play account for listeners. However, he once was given the assignment of covering the Celtics exhibition game against a team from Yugoslavia. For Most, the names of the players from the opposing team were nearly impossible to pronounce, so he improvised.

The broadcast sounded like this: "Rebound by one of the big guys . . . hands off to one of the little guards." He continued to labor, "The big guy with the beard passes off to the little lefty . . . Boy, I'm having trouble with these names!"

•

Once, on a brutal dunk shot, Shaquille O'Neal yanked down the entire basket support system. Teammate Steve Kerr observed, "Sometimes he dunks so hard that you're sure the whole backboard and everything [in the arena] is going to come down." When someone asked Shaq, "You didn't even dunk it that hard today, did you?" his terse reply was, "I dunk all of them hard."

In February of 1992 when the Houston Rockets hosted Charles Barkley and his Phoenix Suns, they ran a special promotion. Any male fan who got his head shaved, a la Barkley, would get two free tickets to the game. Any female fan who cut off all her locks would receive season tickets. Unbelievably, about 200 fans agreed to the shaving, with 12 of them being females.

One of the greatest winning streaks in college history was the one UCLA compiled from January 23, 1971, when they lost to Notre Dame, until almost three years later, when the Fighting Irish snapped their awesome 88 victories in a row run. That streak was 28 games longer than the former Division I record held by the University of San Francisco.

The skein ended on January 19, 1974, when UCLA held a 70–59 lead with just three minutes and thirty-two seconds left on the clock. Unbelievably, the Fighting Irish rattled off 12 unanswered points to take the lead.

The Bruins had the ball, though, and 21 ticks on the clock to win the game. They got the ball to their big man, Bill Walton, but he missed with a mere six seconds left. Three times a UCLA player, crashing the boards, tipped the ball towards the hoop, but the ball never fell through. When Notre Dame's John Shumate snagged the rebound, time ran out and so did the Bruins' streak.

●

During the last few ticks of the clock during game seven of the 1965 Eastern Division Finals, Boston's John Havlicek came up with a play that is still among the biggest ever in NBA play. His Celtics led rival Philadelphia, 110–109, but the 76'ers had the ball.

Hal Greer prepared to inbound the ball, wanting to get it to Wilt Chamberlain, hoping a score by "The Dipper" down low would win it all. When Greer couldn't get the ball to the big man, he attempted to pass to Chet Walker instead. Havlicek, they say, gave Greer the impression his man was open for the pass. Then, in a split second, Havlicek streaked nearer to Walker and flicked the ball to the court where a teammate, Sam Jones, recovered the ball.

Just as baseball fans enjoy the timeless radio call of announcer Russ Hodges who shouted, "The Giants win the pennant" five times when Bobby Thomson hit a dramatic, game-ending homer in 1951, the NBA has this moment. When Havlicek clinched the win, Celtics announcer Johnny Most excitedly blurted, "Havlicek stole the ball. It's all over. Johnny Havlicek stole the ball."

10 LIFE AS AN NBA ROOKIE

Many college stars who have enjoyed huge success at every level of basketball play suddenly hit a restraining wall when they enter the NBA. While it's true some rookies burst onto the professional scene like a meteor, many learn that they have to pay their dues. Here's a look at both the ups and downs in the lives of pro rookies. All quotes are from the players' interview with the author.

Sharpshooter Chuck Person came out of the Auburn Class of '86 and broke into the NBA as the fourth overall draft pick. His story was a happy one, as he went on to win the Rookie of the Year Award in 1986–87, scoring almost 19 ppg.

His first trip through the league, he said, was "just the opposite of what rookies usually go through. You usually have a great first half and struggle in the second half. I kinda struggled the first half and got better the second time around.

"I really didn't have any fears or any revelations about failing or not succeeding because I knew I was going to be a good player in this league and I knew I was going to have a good time doing it." He added, with all the confidence of an Old West gunslinger, "I was never afraid of any player that I stepped on the court against. I'm always thinking I'm the best."

Many rookies come apart due to the hectic travel in the NBA, but Person stated, "I'm very disciplined. I get my rest and I get the proper nutrition." He didn't even find the long NBA season to be a grind. "Well, not for me it didn't because I enjoy it. I love stepping on the court every night, playing and competing against the next guy."

Person added the competition wasn't always easy as veterans constantly test rookies. "It happens all the time. It happened to me, but you have to just accept it and move on." He said that if veteran players sense a rookie can't cope with their hard line tactics, they will continue to use such ploys, including "talking trash," giving rookies a very difficult time. "If veterans feel they're breaking you down, they'll continue to test you."

Person said that, in his case, the NBA players who gave him a rough "education," a sort of Masters Degree in Elbows and Shoves were "Herb Williams, Vern Fleming, and John Long—they gave me the 'extra sauce,' I mean they were on me everyday." The upshot of his story: those men were his *teammates*!

Oscar Robertson was so good, Jerry West was fond of saying, he was never a rookie. Robertson himself felt he adjusted pretty smoothly because he was such a thinker and because he was so confident. Accepting the challenge of playing in the pros, he went on to post a great rookie campaign. In fact, in his debut he chalked up the first of many "triple-doubles" in his career, scoring 21 times, pulling down 12 boards, while dishing out 10 assists.

Jim Loscutoff was a typical rookie when he broke in with the Celtics in 1955. Part of the normalcy of rookie life back then was being awarded a pro contract that carried some prestige, but very little money, a far cry from the kind of loot players earned later in that century. For example, for his first three years in the league Loscutoff earned less money than Larry Bird would later receive for playing in *one game*!

Sometimes a rookie with true talent will still find himself getting very little playing time. Dale Ellis was very much like that. He recalled, "I was playing behind Mark Aguirre and Rolando Blackman. I wasn't going to get many minutes behind a couple of All-Stars."

His big break didn't come until 1986–1987, his fourth year in the NBA. "I was unhappy and asked to be moved; they agreed to trade me." Ellis went from Dallas to Seattle where he blossomed and his court time skyrocketed from about 16 minutes per game (with the Mavs) up to 37-plus minutes.

Thanks to the confidence shown in him by coach Bernie Bickerstaff, Ellis turned in perhaps the greatest one-year turnaround by any pro player ever. Further, when based on improvement of scoring average alone, his jump was the greatest ever. Ellis noted, "By about seven games into the season he [Bickerstaff] built a lot of the offense around me."

By season's end, Ellis had gone from being a 7.1 ppg player to averaging a whopping 24.9 ppg. His assist total took off from 37 to 238 and his rebound total also soared, from 168 to 447. It was no wonder this one-time floundering rookie earned the Most Improved Player of the Year Award in 1986–1987.

Christian Laettner was highly touted when he broke into the pros. When asked if any veterans or coaches on his team were showing him the NBA ropes, he replied, "No. Not really, there hasn't been too much help in that sense from my team and my coaches. They're kind of letting me go through it alone." While that approach is unusual, it can occur.

Laettner realized, "every rookie has to prove himself. Whether against an All-Star veteran or against anyone, you're always going to be challenged, and if it's being challenged in that sense [of testing rookies], so be it."

He also pointed out that expectations placed on players can vary depending upon what team one plays for. His rookie season was spent with a very weak Minnesota Timberwolves squad, one that would win a mere 19 games, second worst in the league. Therefore, he stated, "Here we want ourselves to play well and be in the game at the end of the game. At Duke we were expected to win every time we stepped on the court. So, expectations are a little different."

Danny Ferry's rookie season in the NBA was different than most players in that it was not his first season as a pro. Ferry had played overseas in Italy before returning to the United States to join the Cleveland Cavaliers. He said his first year in the NBA was unlike anything he had ever experienced before. "First of all, the game's a lot different. Obviously the players are a lot more talented.

"Then there's the whole structure of how the game's played with your illegal defenses, and the 24-second clock is really different. Then, along with that, the amount of games and the travel are factors. My first year we didn't have our own plane, and that made a big difference compared to how we have it now. We went on all commercial flights and that made it a lot tougher because of a lot of early wake-ups on game days."

He pointed out that in college he would typically play "anywhere from 33 to 40 games, so time-wise, it's a lot more of a commitment in the NBA, and, rightly, it should be. The season in college is also long—you probably practice a lot more [there] because you don't have as many games [as the 82 in the NBA]. It's a grueling schedule in the NBA and it's more of an emotional thing because of the amount of games and the travel and so on. In the NBA you have to be a lot more emotionally tough." Thus, he felt rookies, unprepared for the rigors of travel, could definitely tire out by the end of the first season.

Autograph Hunting

Danny Ferry believes there's a big difference between college and pro ball in terms of card collecting and autograph hunting. He stated, "There is some card collecting and so on in college, and there are autograph seekers and all that, but it's definitely more intense in the NBA. There are people out waiting before and after the games here. The numbers are much more."

Because he went to a university known for its basketball program, Ferry himself was used to signing autographs as a youth. "There was a lot of it at Duke. I guess a lot of it depends on what school you come from. It was a smaller town, but there was a lot of it."

Chuck Person said that he also felt there was a huge difference between the degree of intensity of autograph hunters in college and in the NBA, saying "there is absolutely no question it's more serious at the pro level.

"The autographs here [NBA] have become big time now with kids and adults alike who come out and try to seek autographs. You have to be professional in what you do because this is a part of the business; you have to accept responsibility."

Lenny Wilkens says that his view on rookie life in the NBA is different than that of more modern players because during his initial season, 1960–1961, "they played a lot of exhibition games. My first years we played about 17. That's just too much." By the time Wilkens made this comment, the league had cut that amount almost exactly in half.

Wilkens continued, "There was a lot of travel and the traveling conditions weren't as good as they are today. It's a tough adjustment for young players sometimes. Some guys adjust right away, for some it takes longer."

One thing Wilkens noticed quickly during his rookie season was the officiating. "It was very good," he said. "The NBA had some of the top officials at that time. I thought the officiating was better than college."

Antonio Harvey, who broke in with the Lakers in 1993, commented, "[Refs] respect guys who have proven they can last and deserve to get breaks on calls. They make you prove you deserve respect on the court. If you play hard and don't walk around with a chip on your shoulder, they'll treat you with respect."

By the way, one rookie said that even the "coaches make it a little rough on you to see how you'll respond, but they try to make you feel comfortable, too."

Typically rookies, even those who were big name players in college, get teased by the veteran players. Rudy Garciduenas, a Los Angeles Lakers trainer, explained a typical prank. "An unsuspecting rookie is called to my room to do an exercise. He gets up on the massage table facing the wall."

At that point veterans sneak into the room to watch the fun unfold. The trainer instructs the rookie to raise his arms then legs, one at a time, as if it was part of his routine. Finally, the punch line: the player is told to bark like a dog. Puzzled, the player obeys, letting out a tentative "ruff." That's the moment the veterans let out their own howls —of laughter!

Everybody's All-American Glenn Robinson became an instant millionaire when the Milwaukee Bucks made him their number one draft pick in 1994. He inked a 10-year contract worth $68 million. Still, as a rookie he was assigned the thankless duty of carrying equipment bags and balls.

As Garciduenas summed it up, "Veterans let rookies know their place. For example, every Laker rookie has to be a sort of servant for a veteran." As such, the "rook" has to fetch the vet's paper and coffee every morning all year long.

When Antonio Harvey looked back on his rookie season as a Laker, he commented, "It was everything I expected, but more." Despite getting hazed, he grinned, "It's pretty cool being a rookie. It's not as bad as people think. We did have to carry bags and uniforms to be washed. Anything a vet didn't want to carry, we had to."

He continued, "We all got nicknames, mostly silly ones fitting our personality." For example, one player earned the name "Roamy." Harvey said, "They did that to tease him that he couldn't learn the plays and he wound up roaming around the court.

"You get messed with a lot, but it's a learning experience. I look at it as paying my dues and it makes you appreciate being a second-year player. Then you get to do the tricks. It's all done in fun."

Rookies are put to shame in other ways. One of the most famous methods of humiliation is a yearly tradition. As Gary Collier, a Cleveland Cavaliers draft pick going into the 1994–1995 campaign, put it, "Once before a practice two rookies had to sing a song [in front of the entire team]. One chose the National Anthem, and the other chose Old MacDonald. It was pretty funny."

Veterans are very clever when it comes to playing practical jokes on the youngsters. For example, when the team is on the road, vets will find out a rookie's room number. Then, full of mischief, they'll order costly room service for themselves, charging the lavish meals to the rookie.

At checkout time, the shocked rook will start to argue with the hotel manager about the enormity of his bill. Usually, though, he winds up paying the bill rather than miss the team bus, as that would cost him cab fare plus a team fine. One has to pity the poor rookie in such a no-win situation.

One of the most popular annual NBA tricks is the surprise they spring on a rookie prior to the start of the first home game of the year. To begin their warm-ups, teams often run onto the court in a long line. Normally they are led onto the playing area by a veteran. However, for this special game a vet will ask a rookie, "How'd you like to lead us out tonight?"

The victim proudly accepts the honor and dashes onto the court with, say, 34,000 eyes focused on him. This is fine, except for one thing: the veterans don't follow his lead. They stay behind snickering at the embarrassed rookie, who looks silly prancing on the court all alone.

In Cleveland they pulled this on Gary Collier who recalled, "When we played Dallas, [star guard] Mark Price asked us rookies if we wanted to lead the team out. By the time we got out there we realized we were the only ones on the court." While he had to feel odd, Collier took the trick in stride. "What do you do with 17,000 people looking at you out there? What did I do? I shot my lay-ups [as if nothing

276

was wrong]. By the time I did that, my teammates joined me." It's all just a way for veterans to jokingly say, "Hey, welcome to the NBA, kid."

Gary Collier, who was a star in college for Tulsa, where he wound up becoming his conference's Player of the Year, said that life in the NBA for a rookie is very difficult. "We play three or four games a week and you travel so much. You might hit a 10-day road trip where you don't even stay in the same hotel room two nights in a row. That really wears on you. It's not all glamorous like people think. Still, it keeps you going to know you're doing something you really love."

Sadly, the Cavs cut him just four days prior to the start of the season. A player who had averaged 23 points a game in college found life in the NBA to be a matter of "you either cut it or you don't." As a matter of fact, he never spent one minute of time on a regular season NBA court.

When Trevor Winter played in the lowly International Basketball Association, he was paid $250 for his 21-game stay there. In 1999, he was a rookie with the Timberwolves, earning the minimum pay of $287,500 that season. To him that was big money, but when he glanced over at Kevin Garnett he happened to see the numbers on his pay stub. Garnett was getting the first installment of his $14,000,000 salary for the year. Winter later told sportswriters, "I got about what they took out of [his] check for Medicaid."

11 LEGENDARY COACHES

*When the NBA turned 50 years of age, it not only
celebrated its best players it selected the 10 best coaches
in the annals of the league. The Pantheon-like list was made
up of: Lenny Wilkens, Red Holzman, Red Auerbach,
Phil Jackson, Chuck Daly, Pat Riley, Don Nelson,
Bill Fitch, Jack Ramsay, and John Kundla. Read about
these coaches and some influential college coaches.*

As a player, Lenny Wilkens didn't think he was a great
prospect to make it in the NBA. Why, he didn't even try out
for his high school team in 10th and 11th grade. Wilkens was
dead wrong about his future. After starring at Providence,
he did make it as a great guard—few men handled and
passed the ball as well as he did. By the time he retired from
the NBA, he stood #2 on the all-time assists list.

Wilkens clearly knew what the game was all about, once commenting about guard play, "I enjoyed being a point guard because I like running the show, controlling the tempo of the game, and getting the right people involved at the right time."

Such talent led to a new phase of his life on the court. Late in his career he served rare double duty, playing the point guard spot while also coaching the team. That paved the way for a great clipboard career, coaching numerous teams such as the Cleveland Cavaliers, Portland Trail Blazers, Atlanta Hawks, New York Knicks, and the Seattle Supersonics, where he won the title in 1979. He became the winningest coach in NBA annals.

Wilkens is the only man to spend 30 years as a head coach. He is also the only man honored twice by the NBA. He was selected as one of the greatest 50 players of all-time and one of the best 10 coaches ever.

Wilkens also became one of only two men (the other was UCLA legend John Wooden) inducted into the Hall of Fame on two occasions (in 1989 for his playing prowess and in 1998 for his coaching ability).

Paul Silas, who played under Wilkens and later went on to become a head coach in the NBA, praised his former mentor. "The thing about Lenny is that when things are going badly, he doesn't point the finger at anybody. He just keeps working."

As the 20th century came to an end, one of the most famous and successful coaches in the NBA was Phil Jackson. Few men can boast of multiple NBA titles, but Jackson, with wins in 1991, 1992, 1993, 1996, 1997, 1998, 2000, 2001, and 2002, is in that elite club of coaches.

It would seem the term "three-peat" was invented for Jackson and his crews of hoopsters. In addition to that, in nine seasons with the Bulls his team not only averaged 61 regular season wins per year, they also won six championships.

The first six of his championship rings came when he guided the Chicago Bulls of the Michael Jordan era, supported mainly by Scottie Pippen. His next three titles came as the coach of the Los Angeles Lakers and their talented group of stars, including Shaquille O'Neal.

Another huge Laker star, Kobe Bryant, said of his former coach, "Sometimes you might not know exactly what he's talking about, but you still listen." Respect comes to coaches when players know their leader can guide them to the playoffs and perhaps yet another NBA title.

Boston Celtic coach Arnold "Red" Auerbach also owns nine NBA crowns. In his case, forget the term "three-peat" because he actually led his team to eight consecutive titles from 1959 through 1966 to go along with a title won in 1957!

Auerback was very demanding, but it paid off for stars such as Bill Russell, John Havlicek (such a fine athlete he was drafted by the Cleveland Browns as a wide receiver), and Bob Cousy, because they won division titles 10 times from 1956 and 1966, Auerbach's final one on the Boston bench.

Auerbach's trademark mannerism was lighting up a cigar while sitting and observing the game. He would do so at the moment he was convinced his Celtics would win the contest. Some observers thought the move was arrogant, others felt it was unhealthy, but in Boston this man was king.

Another Red—Red Holzman—also became a legendary NBA coach, although with the New York Knicks. Holzman was born about three years after Auerbach, and also in New York City.

Holzman loved to stress the concept of "team basketball," and his unselfish championship teams of 1970 and 1973 were known for their brand of play which featured many stars, not just one superstar. Holzman's most notable players included Willis Reed, Dave DeBusschere, Walt Frazier, and Bill Bradley.

After winning a dramatic and highly emotional championship in a grueling seven-game series in 1970, Holzman was honored as the Coach of the Year. Later the team retired a jersey in his honor. Since he was a coach who certainly did not wear a uniform number on the bench, the Knicks went with 613, the highest jersey number ever retired, to symbolize his win total with the team.

Detroit fans loved the ride that coach Chuck Daly and his Pistons took them on in 1989 and 1990. They won back-to-back titles and did so with a blue-collar coach.

Daly had paid his basketball dues, moving up the ranks as a high school coach, a college coach, and an NBA championship coach. At the time of his trophy winning campaigns, only four other men had won consecutive titles. Daly had, in fact, guided his Pistons to the playoff nine seasons in a row.

•

A former member of the Rockets, Lakers, and Suns, Pat Riley was hardly a star player, even though he had starred in college with the Kentucky Wildcats.

Riley found his niche as an NBA coach. Few men have more regular season or playoff victories than the dapper Riley does. Over a seven-year span from 1981–1982 to 1987–1988, his Lakers won four championship rings, the best string of success since the glory days of the Red Auerbach Celtics.

The man voted Coach of the Year in 1990, 1993, and 1997 had enjoyed success early, leading his Lakers to a title in 1982 as a rookie coach. Additionally, he won it all again in 1985, 1987, and 1988.

After winning his first crown, he joked that he was so exhausted he suffered from "brain drain." He added, "I dug down for everything I could find. I need four months to rest up."

Even after departing Los Angeles, Riley still ran a winning program. His teams in Los Angeles, New York, and Miami all won 60 or more games under his guidance on at least one occasion.

Riley was the only man to win the Coach of the Year Award with three different teams.

Jack Ramsay was considered to be a fine teacher of the game, and his teams played the game as it was meant to be played. Perhaps that was never more true than in 1976–1977, the year his Portland Trail Blazers executed so well, they won it all.

When he hung his clipboard up for good, only six coaches owned more NBA victories than his 864, earning him a spot in the Hall of Fame.

Don Nelson's first great playing moments in the NBA revolved around his membership with the dynastic Celtics. When he came aboard as a coach, he was accustomed to winning—and that's exactly what he continued to do. By the time he had recorded over 900 wins, he stood #9 on the all-time win list.

According to *The Official NBA Encyclopedia*, "No one has been more creative than [Nelson]. . . And if ever there was a bench leader who could take advantage of a rule to benefit his team, then Nelson was the guy."

The coaching career of John Kundla goes back so far, fans today either don't remember him, or don't tend to give him the credit he deserves. Coming out of the high school coaching ranks, he worked with George Mikan and took the Lakers (then Minneapolis) to the top in 1948. Over the next six seasons he won five more titles, this time in a different league called the Basketball Association of America.

With his won-loss percentage of almost .600, it's no surprise to discover Kundla was elected into the Hall of Fame.

Always handy with a witty one-liner, Bill Fitch was very popular. He began his career as a college coach, but hardly at a big-time program (Coe College in Iowa). Over his 25 years in the NBA, he steered four teams to a total of 944 wins, which placed him third on the all-time list.

Fitch's shining moment was winning the title with the Larry Bird Celtics in 1981. A two-time Coach of the Year, he was also the guiding force behind the Cleveland Cavaliers' "Miracle of Richfield" in 1975–1976 in which the lowly Cavs stormed all the way to the Eastern Conference Finals.

•

John Wooden, the legendary UCLA coach, began his playing days in the hotbed of basketball, the state of Indiana. There, in Martinsville, he helped his high school win the state championship. His next stop was Purdue, where he captured All-American honors three times and was named the College Player of the Year in 1932. He was, in fact, the first player to gain All-American status three times. Staying in-state, he began coaching for Indiana State University. In 1948 he became coach of the UCLA Bruins. He would coach the team to ten NCAA Men's Basketball Championships, including seven in a row.

Under coach Mike Kyzyzewski, winning has become routine for the Duke Blue Devils. To illustrate his impact, consider Duke's 1994–1995 season. Kyzyzewski guided the team to a 9–3 record, but when health problems plagued him, he couldn't complete the year. The Blue Devils floundered the remainder of the year, going 4–15. Then, upon his return, victories flowed once again, and by 1996–1997 his record soared to 24–9.

The following season, Duke racked up a 32-win campaign, and the next year they went a sizzling 37–2, ending the season number one in the Associated Press poll. In fact, that team was the first one ever to enjoy a perfect 16–0 season in the prestigious Atlantic Coast Conference (ACC).

When Kyzyzewski was just one game shy of his 700th career victory, a level reached by only 15 coaches ever, he spoke of the importance of each and every win. "I remember coaching at Army," he began, "and if we won one, we were lucky. So I told myself I would appreciate each game."

Bobby Knight holds a unique distinction among college basketball coaches. Through 2004, he was the only coach ever to win the NCAA tournament, the NIT tournament, the Olympics, and even the Pan Am (American) Games.

12 COLLEGE TEAM NICKNAMES

Team nicknames are carefully selected. Usually the names conjure up images of strength or speed. A name like Panthers is a rugged one, a name that can inspire or even instill fear in opponents. That's why a college would never go with a name such as the Purdue Pumpkins or the DePaul Daisies. The college basketball ranks are full of great, colorful, odd and interesting nicknames.

At least three teams changed their nicknames out of respect to Native American Indians. Miami of Ohio used to be known as the Redskins but switched to Red Hawks. The Marquette Warriors became the Golden Eagles and the Redmen of St. John's now go by Red Storm.

In a seemingly odd alteration, Stanford went from Cardinals, plural, to simply "Cardinal."

Arizona State has been proud of its two-word nickname, the Sun Devils, for years. The University of Mississippi has been known as the Rebels, but also Ole Miss. Next, there are the Tar Heels of the University of North Carolina, the Amazin' Aggies of New Mexico State University, the Wake Forest Demon Deacons, Texas Christian Horned Frogs, and the Nittany Lions of Penn State.

Interestingly, two teams are nicknamed the Wolf Pack, but North Carolina State spells the name as one word, while Nevada spells it as two words.

College Nickname Contest

For some reason, many teams have placed a verb in their nickname. For example, there is the Fighting Irish of Notre Dame. Can you match the college up with its nickname?

1. Campbell
2. Marshall
3. University of Delaware
4. Hostra
5. University of Illinois
6. Western Illinois
7. University of Nevada at Las Vegas
8. St. Mary's College
9. University of Southwestern Louisiana

A. Fighting Leathernecks
B. Runnin' Rebels (Rebs)
C. Galloping Gaels
D. Fighting Camels
E. Thundering Herd
F. Ragin' Cajuns
G. Flying Dutchmen
H. Fightin' Blue Hens
I. Fighting' Illini

The answers are: 1. D (Campbell Fighting Camels); 2. E (Marshall Thundering Herd); 3. H (Fightin' Blue Hens); 4. G (Flying Dutchmen); 5. I (University of Illinois Fightin' Illini); 6. A (Western Illinois Fighting Leathernecks); 7. B (University of Nevada at Las Vegas Runnin' Rebels); 8. C (St. Mary's College Galloping Gaels); and 9. F (Ragin' Cajuns).

College Nicknames Dealing with Color

Colors are also featured often in college nicknames. Can you match the college with its colorful nickname?

1. University of Bridgeport	A. Yellow Jackets
2. Colgate	B. Green Wave
3. Dartmouth	C. The Red Flash
4. DePaul	D. Rainbows
5. Duke	E. Purple Eagles
6. University of Evansville	F. Red Raiders
7. University of Maine	G. Purple Knights
8. Georgia Tech	H. Scarlet Knights

293

9. University of Hawaii	I. Blue Demons
10. Middle Tennessee State University	J. Black Bears
11. Niagara	K. Big Green
12. Rutgers	L. Purple Aces
13. Texas Tech	M. Red Raiders
14. St. Francis (of Pennsylvania)	N. Blue Raiders
15. Tulane	O. Blue Devils

The answers are: 1. G (University of Bridgeport Purple Knights); 2. F (Colgate Red Raiders); 3. K (Dartmouth Big Green); 4. I (DePaul Blue Demons); 5. O (Duke Blue Devils); 6. L (University of Evansville Purple Aces); 7. J (University of Maine Black Bears); 8. A (Georgia Tech Yellow Jackets); 9. D (University of Hawaii Rainbows); 10. N (Middle Tennessee State University Blue Raiders); 11. E (Niagara Purple Eagles); 12. H (Rutgers Scarlet Knights; 13. M (Texas Tech Red Raiders); 14. C (St. Francis of Pennsylvania The Red Flash); and 15. B (Tulane Green Wave).

The University of Akron goes by the name of Zips, and the Loyola Ramblers is also an unusual name. Manhattan College is known as the Jaspers, but one of the oddest nicknames of all belongs to the Vandals of the University of Idaho.

That also holds true for the Richmond Spiders. Although many people are certainly afraid of Spiders, that name hardly seems to fit on, say, a football field or a basketball court. Likewise, the nickname of St. Peter's College in New Jersey is quite different—the Peacocks.

When it comes to nicknames that hardly inspire awe or fear, Virginia Tech may rank number one, as they are the Gobblers.

Some nicknames are words few people have even heard of. For instance, Georgetown is dubbed the Hoyas. Next there are the Billikens of the University of St. Louis and the Salukis of Southern Illinois University.

The nickname of the Terrapins of Maryland requires some explanation, but, once heard, the name is quite logical. A terrapin is a turtle that can be found in the state of Maryland.

Perhaps the most logical name of all belongs to Lehigh, a college that produces many engineers. Guess what? They go by the nickname of Engineers. Next is Jacksonville, located in Florida, and known as the Dolphins.

Massachusetts is a state rich in the history of the American Revolution, so the University of Massachusetts chose the nickname the Minutemen. The Citadel team goes by the name of Cadets, although they are sometimes also referred to as the Bulldogs. By the way, the basketball team for the United States Military Academy at West Point is also nicknamed the Cadets, while the Naval Academy team goes by Midshipmen. The Dayton Flyers makes sense as that city, home to Orville and Wilbur Wright, helped give birth to flight.

Another name tied in with history belongs to the Sooners of Oklahoma. The story there is simple: When the state opened up some areas of land for settlers to claim and then live on, they held a "land run." At exactly noon on April 22nd of 1889, a cannon boom signaled the start of the run and people dashed to claim some of the territory. However, some people cheated. Wanting to beat others to desirable locations for homesteads, they entered early and hid until the legal time of entry. Those people became known as "sooners."

The University of Pennsylvania Quakers makes sense for a nickname, as do the names Pepperdine (at Malibu, California) Waves and the Puget Sound Loggers in Washington, a state famed for its rich forests. Similarly, West Virginia took on the geographic nickname of Mountaineers, and Western Kentucky teams are called the Hilltoppers. Finally, since Stetson hats are famous, it makes sense that Stetson University is called the Hatters.

13 PLAYER TIDBITS

Here are behind-the-scenes glimpses of past and present college and professional ballplayers.

One of the greatest athletes on earth was Michael Jordan, a ten-time scoring champ and winner of six NBA titles. Throughout his NBA career he led his Chicago Bulls to title after title while averaging just over 30 ppg, good for 32,292 career points.

Even Jordan, a five-time MVP, struggled when he tried to become a two-sport athlete. When he attempted to find glory in the world of baseball, his quest began with a minor league team known as the Birmingham Barons.

In 1994, Jordan did manage to compile a rather impressive 13-game hitting streak while hitting .327. He had even been successful in 11 of his first 17 stolen base attempts. By June 1st, though, his batting average had plummeted below

.200 and it became clear that the legend of the courts wouldn't cut it on the baseball diamonds.

•

Even though he played for the losing Los Angeles Clippers in 2004–2005, Bobby Simmons was what the Associated Press called "a runaway winner" of the Most Improved Player trophy. The next two top vote getters were Dwayne Wade of the Miami Heat (44 first-place votes behind Simmons' 59) and Tayshaun Prince of the Detroit Pistons (with one less first-place vote than Wade). In a nice gesture, the 24-year-old Simmons credited his coach, "I never had the opportunity to show what I can do. Coach [Mike] Dunleavy gave me that opportunity."

Simmons improved his scoring output from 7.8 ppg to 16.4, more than doubling what he had managed the year before as he established career highs for scoring, rebounds, assists, steals, and even minutes played.

Simmons joined other big name winners of this award, including Jalen Rose, Tracy McGrady, Jermaine O'Neal and Gilbert Arenas.

At the start of the 2004 season, John Thompson III made history when he coached his first game for the Georgetown Hoyas. Even though he lost his debut to the Temple Owls, his appearance as a Division I coach made him and his father, John Thompson, Jr., just the seventh father-son combination to coach at the uppermost level of the college ranks at the same school.

•

Dave DeBusschere of the Detroit Pistons and the New York Knicks was one of the game's toughest defenders. He made the first team on the All-Defense team each season from 1969 to 1974.

This multi-talented player was able to make it not only in the NBA but at the major league level in baseball as well. After playing both sports in college at the University of Detroit, he signed contracts with two teams in that same part of the country: the Pistons and the Chicago White Sox. So, for his first two NBA seasons, he also played big league baseball.

DeBusschere lasted two years in baseball at the major league level, posting a 3–4 record as a pitcher, but he clearly was a much better hoopster.

Chuck Connors also played both professional baseball and basketball. He spent one game of the 1949 season with the Dodgers and was back to the majors for 66 more contests in 1951 with the Cubs, hitting only .238 lifetime. In basketball, the 6' 6" Connors played only 67 professional contests.

●

Del Rice carved out a solid 17-year major league baseball career and was an All-Star catcher for the St. Louis Cardinals. Rice also played for a short time in basketball's old NBL.

●

Dave Winfield wound up being a baseball Hall of Famer, but he was actually drafted by four different pro teams from three different sports. The San Diego Padres signed him to play baseball, but the NFL's Minnesota Vikings also wanted him, as did the Utah Stars of the ABA and the Atlanta Hawks as well.

●

The 6' 5" Ron Reed lasted 19 years in the majors as a pitcher. He racked up 146 wins and 103 saves from 1966–1984. He spent two seasons in the NBA (8.1 ppg lifetime) when he was doing double duty, playing two sports at the professional level at the same time.

Dick Groat was an All-American in 1951–1952 as a college hoop star at Duke. One year earlier, he had set an NCAA single season scoring record (831).

Groat was drafted into the NBA, where he played for Fort Wayne in 1953. There he averaged almost 12 ppg.

Groat's main fame came as a baseball player. He was a rookie in 1952, but wasn't back in the majors until 1955. As the shortstop for the 1960 World Champion Pittsburgh Pirates, he led the National League in hitting with a fine .325 batting average. Further, he was named the league's MVP that wonderful season.

Later Groat returned to the world of basketball as the executive vice-president of the Pittsburgh Condors of the ABA.

Danny Ainge was a star for the Celtics during the 1980s, although his best scoring output was with the Sacramento Kings (17.9 ppg in 1989–1990). A fine all-round athlete at Brigham Young, he was good enough in baseball to spend 211 games with the Toronto Blue Jays from 1979–1981.

Ainge was versatile on defense, playing shortstop, second base, third base, and the outfield, but hit only .220.

●

Bud Grant carved out a fine career as the head coach in the National Football League. However, he also spent time in pro basketball. He stuck close to familiar grounds as he played his college ball at the University of Minnesota, became the field general of the Minnesota Vikings, and spent two seasons on the court with the Minneapolis Lakers.

●

The 6' 8" Gene Conley was a pitcher from 1952–1963 who earned 91 big league victories. In basketball he played in the NBA in 1952, making him a two-sport rookie that year. He did not return to the NBA until 1958, where he stayed until 1964.

Conley played for both the Boston Celtics and Boston Braves in 1952 and spent part of 1961 with the Celtics and the Boston Red Sox.

One of the most interesting tales of two-sport players belongs to Charlie Ward who, many feel, is the best college football player ever to play in the NBA. At Florida State, he was the starting quarterback, and took the Seminoles to a national title in 1993. He monopolized collegiate awards, winning the coveted Heisman Trophy, the Sullivan Award, and the Maxwell Award. He was also named College Football Player of the Year by *The Sporting News*.

At 6'2", Ward also played basketball for four years at Florida State, teaming up with future NBA players Doug Edwards, Sam Cassell, and Bob Sura. In his senior year, he saw hardwood action in his first game of the season only 15 days after winning MVP honors as a quarterback at the Orange Bowl.

When it came time to pick the sport he'd play as a pro, Ward elected basketball over football and was drafted by the New York Knicks in the first round of the 1994 NBA Draft.

Ward was so athletic that even though he didn't play baseball in college he was drafted by the Milwaukee Brewers in the 1993 free agent draft and by the New York Yankees in 1994.

304

Foreign-Born Players

While it is hardly unusual to see foreign-born players make it big in the NBA in the late 20th and into the 21st century, at one time it was an oddity. Here are some interesting facts about past and present NBA players.

Tim Duncan was a great free-style distance swimmer as a youth in his native Virgin Islands. When a hurricane wiped out the pool where he trained, he turned his attention to the roundball.

Patrick Ewing was born in Kingston, Jamaica, the same island that also produced Rumeal Robinson. Mychal Thompson comes from Nassau, Bahamas.

Ewing's fellow Georgetown graduate Dikembe Mutombo hailed from Zaire in Africa. The towering Manute Bol was born in Sudan. Famous deluxe imports from Nigeria include Hakeem Olajuwon, Michael Olowokandi, and Obinna Ekezie.

Luc Longley made it to the NBA by way of the Australia. Rony Seikaly was born in Lebanon, and fellow big man Zydrunas Ilgauskas (some just call him "Z") is Lithuanian.

•

Norm Baker and Gino Sovran were the first Canadians to play in the NBA. They entered the league in 1946–1947, the same year as Hank Biasatti, the first Italian-born player, who played for the old Toronto Huskies franchise. Ernie Vandeweghe, another Canadian, became an NBA player in 1949–1950. Much later, Steve Nash and Jamaal Magloire joined the league via Canada.

•

Tito Horford and Felipe Lopez are both from the Dominican Republic, while Butch Lee, once the College Player of the Year, is from Puerto Rico. Haiti produced Olden Polynice.

Vitaly Potapenko was born in the Ukraine, and Toni Kukoc is from Croatia. Gheorghe Muresan was an incredible sight at 7' 7" and hailed from Romania. There has even been a player born in Egypt. Alaa Abdelnaby, the man whose name comes first alphabetically in the basketball encyclopedia, played for several NBA teams, including the Philadelphia 76'ers and Sacramento Kings.

Probably when most fans think of foreign born players, they concentrate on Europe and even Asia. As of March 15, 2004, NBA team rosters featured 67 international players from 33 countries and territories. These include 2004 All-Stars Andrei Kirilenko (Russia), Dirk Nowitzki (Germany), and Peja Stojakovic (listed as being from Serbia and Montenegro).

Due to his size (and later for an especially funny television commercial), Yao Ming made headlines in 2002 when the 7' 6" giant, with a homeland of China, entered the NBA.

The first surge of talented European players entered the NBA in the mid to late 1980s and included players such as Drazen Petrovic (from Croatia), Sarunas Marciulionis (Lithuania), Swen Nater, and Rik Smits, sometimes called "Dutch Boy in the Paint" (from Holland), Detlef Schrempf and Uwe Blab (both hailing from Germany), Alexander Volkov (Ukraine), and Vlade Divac (Serbia-Montenegro).

The WNBA drew players from around the world, too. Elena Baranova made her way to the league via Russia, while China gave the WNBA Haixia Zheng. Meanwhile, Michele Timms came from Australia, where she had been an Olympian.

From High School to the Pros

While players leaving high school and going directly to the NBA are no longer rare, at one time such an event was headline material.

The first men to "go pro" directly out of high school date back to the 1974 and 1975 era. On August 28, 1974, the media reported the fact that Moses Malone, who had just recently graduated from high school in Petersburg, Virginia, had been signed by the Utah Stars of the ABA. In less than a year, Bill Willoughby and Darryl Dawkins joined this select group of players.

In June of 2001, a new barrier was broken when 19-year-old Kwame Brown became the first high school player to be the first overall pick in the draft. Moments later, fellow high schooler Tyson Chandler followed Brown as the second pick.

Insights on the Game

Marty Blake, one of the most respected NBA experts (presently, he is the NBA Director of Scouting), and a man who has been involved with the draft for around 50 years, addressed what it takes to build a winner. "You win with talent. You [also] gotta' have role players."

Blake noted, too, that as a rule a team can't win without a force at the center position and "big guys take longer to develop [than, say, guards]." So, he feels it's wise to be patient with such players, often waiting an extra two or three years.

Blake said successful teams have "to try to develop their own talent." To do so means drafting wisely and that's not always easy. As he pointed out, "The draft isn't an exact science. Twelve men got picked ahead of Karl Malone for that matter."

When asked his opinion on the theory that big men taking longer to make it in the NBA, Nate Thurmond observed, "Some big men take longer—some do, some don't. But if you're good, you're good. Take a look at that guy from L.S.U.," he said, referring to a then-young Shaquille O'Neal. "You can't tell me it'll take him time." It didn't.

The O'Neal Era was ushered in when he became the first rookie ever to walk away with the Player of the Week Award—in his first week in the league! In his 1992 debut, he grabbed 18 boards, the best first-game rebounding effort since Bill Walton pulled down 24 in 1974.

Notre Dame superstar Austin Carr said that it takes more than talent to win. "Match-ups are the key in the NBA," he said, pointing out that a team must be able to handle opponents with "fast lineups, strong lineups, and big rebounding lineups." Often a good team picks up one new player and such an addition gives the squad "more flexibility [so that a team will] not be caught with any match-ups [they] can't handle."

Carr gave an example of the time a solid Cleveland Cavs team acquired an aging but still productive and intimidating 6' 11" Nate Thurmond in 1975–1976. Jim Chones was the Cavs starting center but, like any player, would need rest on occasion. Carr recalled, "We were 6–11 when Nate came [via a trade]. Within a month's time, we turned it around." The Cavs went 43 and 22 the rest of the way to capture the Central Division title.

Carr said another reason the Cavs became a winner that season was they were 10 players deep. Having a good bench is yet another NBA key.

Carr added one more important factor—a young team must be "mature enough to withstand the ebbs and flows of the NBA season." If a team is too young, with, for instance, no stabilizing veterans, they may play well, but fall short of playoff success.

If a young team begins to win and surprises the league with their play, there can be a surprising negative to that the following season. Carr said that a team that goes fairly deep in the playoffs will find that if they were "just one step short last year, that next step to get there is a huge step. Everyone will be shooting at them." It would be, he said, "constant pressure." And to beat teams in the playoffs often means "overcoming a team that's done it [won titles] before." Such teams don't roll over; therefore, moving up the ladder is tougher than most fans realize.

Rick Barry told *Basketball Digest* that for a team to blend and play well together, "you've got to subjugate your own talent to bring out the best in a teammate." "You can't win with a team full of jealousy, so you've got to make sure that everyone feels he is contributing."

To put it mildly, the draft process can be inexact. Proof of this occurred in 1983, when the Houston Rockets selected Ralph Sampson as the number one overall choice. The Rockets' team president called Sampson "the player of the century," but due to problems such as injuries, the 7' 4" center never quite made it as big as had been expected.

When healthy, Sampson did put up some good numbers (he enjoyed two 20+ ppg seasons) and he did cop the Rookie of the Year Award. However, by 1989–1990 he was the lowly 12th man on the roster and could muster only 4.2 ppg with an anemic .372 FG%, miserable for anyone, but especially for a center.

Likewise, Sam Bowie was the second overall selection in 1984, with Portland picking him over Michael Jordan! The 7' 1" Kentucky grad wound up with more injuries than Evel Knieval, while Jordan went on to become a living legend.

314

Jersey Numbers That Have Been Retired

Other than induction into the Hall of Fame, the ultimate way to honor a player is to retire his jersey number. Several years ago Boston Celtic official, David Zuccaro, explained how a player is selected. "There really is no specific criteria. Red [Auerbach] always initiates the idea [here]. The owners and general manager then add their input."

It sounded like, as a rule, if Auerbach gave a thumb's up sign the deserving candidate got rubber-stamped and his jersey would be raised into the old Boston Gardens rafters.

In Philadelphia, the 76'ers honored Dave Zinkoff with a banner that featured not a numeral, but a likeness of a microphone. Only veteran announcers such as Zinkoff and Boston's Johnny Most get such kudos.

"The Zink," as Zinkoff was known, went back to the days of the Philadelphia Warriors and was famous for electrifying fans with trademark descriptions such as, "Basket by Cham-ber-lain."

Zinkoff coined such phrases as "Dipper Dunk" (for a Chamberlain slam); "Two for Shue" (a Gene Shue bucket); "Gola goal" (for a Tom Gola hoop); and "Ohl goal" (when Don Ohl sank a field goal).

Another odd case was that of Milwaukee's Sidney Moncrief. His #4 was retired around mid-season in 1990, less than a year after he had proclaimed, "I just decided I'd had enough. I was burned out."

Just three days before the start of the following season, Moncrief asked the Atlanta Hawks if he could show up for a tryout. He not only made the team, he did well as a role player, making him the only active player to have a retired uniform.

When the Celtics retired Larry Bird's jersey on February 4, 1993, they decided to do so in a very special ceremony. Never before had such an event been staged on its own—normally a pre-game or halftime ceremony would be held to honor a player. This time a two-and-a-half hour presentation, with one ticket going for a lofty

$575, was needed to praise Bird and to hoist his #33 jersey into the coveted Rafter Heaven at Boston Garden. They even presented the legend with a piece of the famed parquet floor.

Bird spoke of how much he loved the game. "I never put on a uniform to play a game. I put on a uniform to win." He went on to say, "I'll miss working the pick-and-roll with Robert Parish. I'll miss getting the ball in low to Kevin McHale and watching him go to work. I'll miss those backdoor passes from Dennis Johnson. Most of all, believe it or not, I'll miss the fans."

Respected rival Magic Johnson lauded Bird, "I feared you more than anyone else, because I knew that if there was a little time left on the clock. . . you know, one point one, half a second. . . you would find a way to win that game." He went on to state, "Larry, you only told me one lie. You said there will be another Larry Bird. Larry, there will never, ever be another Larry Bird. You take that to the bank. I love you. I respect you. I admire you."

The Sacramento Kings actually retired a jersey for the fans. They showed their appreciation for their fan support by retiring a #6 to represent the idea of the crowd as being a sort of inspirational "sixth man" on the team.

Some experts say the greatest player of all-time was, almost unbelievably, a man who few fans ever heard of. The player was 6' 2" Earl "The Goat" Manigault of Harlem, New York.

Local lore has it his vertical leap was an unheard of 50 inches. Friends would place quarters on top of the backboard and Manigault could fly up and gather a quick and easy "pay day."

Manigault was truly a playground legend in New York, but not only did not make it to the pros, he never made it to the college ranks either, since he never graduated from high school.

Manigault passed away in 1998, but his name is still uttered with awe in New York.

Television and radio announcers were as amused as they were confused when they scanned the NBA's media data, which included a guide for players with names that were difficult to pronounce. To help them handle Detlef Schrempf's name, the guide listed "DET-lef" for the first name. So far, so good. However, as for his surname, it merely spelled out "SCHREMPF," as if that was sufficient clarification!

A Flip of the Coin

Starting with the 1966 draft, the two last-place teams from the league's two divisions took part in a coin flip. The lowly team that won the toss would choose first. That system lasted until 1985 when the NBA began its lottery. Still, more than a few teams' fates depended upon a simple flip of a coin:

The most famous case had to be in 1969 when two teams realized that the future could be as bright as a nova. The Milwaukee Bucks and the Phoenix Suns were both only one year old and, naturally, were struggling as infant franchises. A Phoenix official called "heads" and was dismayed when the coin landed showing "tails."

Milwaukee won, selected UCLA sensation Lew Alcindor, and turned their team around in a heartbeat. The Suns wound up with Neal Walk, who never made in big in the NBA (12.6 ppg lifetime).

When they won the NBA championship two years later, with the help of an aging Oscar Robertson, the

Bucks became the quickest team (from their inception to the year of their championship) in a major pro sports to cop a title.

Five years after the Alcindor gift to the Bucks, another UCLA center, Bill Walton, was "won" in a coin toss. This time it was the Portland Trailblazers who would benefit big time, eventually winning an NBA crown with Walton. The 76'ers took Marvin Barnes as the second pick and wound up empty-handed. Barnes refused to sign with Philadelphia and went to St. Louis in the ABA.

In 1979 the toss was between Chicago and the New Orleans Jazz, but the Lakers wound up owning the Jazz's pick. When the Bulls lost the flip, they had to settle for David Greenwood, yet another UCLA hoopster. He lasted with them for six seasons, enjoying five decent ones, but never averaged better than the 16.3 ppg he produced in his rookie season. In the meantime, the Lakers took none other than superstar Magic Johnson.

The final coin flip was won by the Houston Rockets, who immediately announced their pick was Hakeem Olajuwon. Like Abdul-Jabbar, Walton, and Johnson, the standout center would lead his team to glory. In his case, he helped Houston to back-to-back championships.

The second man to go was Sam Bowie, signed by Portland. Due to several factors, the 7' 1" college megastar at Kentucky never panned out. After an adequate rookie season, he played in just 63 games over his next three seasons. His career scoring average stood at 10.9 ppg, less than half of Olajuwon's 23.1 ppg.

In the late 1970s, the biggest name in woman's basketball was Ann Meyers, a four-time All-American at UCLA, where she eclipsed 12 of the women's team's 13 records. She went on to earn a silver medal for her play on the U.S. Olympic team in 1976.

Meyers made headlines when the Indiana Pacers signed her to a $50,000 contract, making her the first woman to sign an NBA deal. The contract allowed her to pocket the cash, even though she didn't make it past the team's tryouts.

When Meyers, who married baseball Hall of Famer Don Drysdale, was inducted into the roundball Hall of Fame, she spoke of how she "idolized my brother David and always tagged along with him." Her older brother was also a UCLA grad, and he lasted four years with the Bucks.

The NBA made it clear it wasn't ready for a female star. It still isn't, although a pro league for women, the WNBA, did come into play.

Despite all of her accomplishments, most men in the NBA were not at all supportive concerning the drafting of a female. Pat Williams, then the general manager of Philadelphia, stated, "This is the zenith in promotions. My reaction is it has to be a publicity-oriented gimmick." Boston's Red Auerbach added, "It's still a man's game." He said that Meyers was a power forward when playing with women but would be considered "a mini guard" in the NBA.

Two of the greatest centers ever, Wilt Chamberlain and Bill Russell, were huge rivals, facing each other in countless big games.

While Russell's Celtics teams won more NBA titles, "The Stilt" actually outplayed Russell time and time again. Statistically it looked like this: In 142 matchups, Chamberlain averaged 28.7 points and exactly 28.7 rebounds. On 24 of those occasions, he had 35 or more points, with 28 rebounds or better. These are staggering numbers.

Perhaps Chamberlain's best statistical output versus Russell was the time he rained down some 62 points while yanking 28 rebounds.

None of this should be shocking, as Chamberlain once averaged an unbelievable 27.2 rpg for an entire season (1960–1961) and once crashed the boards for yet another record, 55 in a single game!

It's a bit difficult to believe now, but Magic Johnson's great Laker teammate Kareem Abdul-Jabbar actually said, "I had doubts at first [about Johnson's skill], but I talked to [former Los Angeles coach] Jack McKinney during the summer before his rookie season and Jack kept saying, 'Magic has such unique talent, you're going to love it. We'll be able to run all the time and nobody's going to be able to just concentrate on you.' And he was absolutely right."

When Magic broke the assist record held by Oscar Robertson, he joked, calling his parents "Magic Makers," and tearfully, yet happily, recalled the days of his youth in Michigan. "I thought about all the times we played 'shirts' and 'skins,' hoping one day to get into the NBA. I cried for all the times I shoveled snow off the walk and practiced hook shots with my dad. I cried for my dad. He's the one; he's the only reason I'm here. He explained to me how to share the basketball."

Kareem Abdul-Jabbar, who played with both Oscar Robertson and Magic Johnson, was diplomatic in comparing the two. "I guess the bottom line on them is about the same. They were both so skillful at getting you the ball in scoring position.

"I think the differences of style were very dramatic, though, and make for an interesting contrast. Magic is very flamboyant; he enjoys bringing out the skill and showmanship aspects of the game, and he's very demonstrative. Oscar was the exact opposite; he just threw the ball very simply, and he didn't get very emotional about it. But they were both very consistent, and had the best eyes of anybody I've ever played with."

Abdul-Jabbar concluded by saying, "I don't think Magic could have been a guard, though, if it hadn't been for Oscar. Oscar was the first guy who came from the front line—he'd been a forward all his life—to point guard, and his ball handling, rebounding, and shooting skill enabled him to play anywhere on the court. Magic took that and brought it to another level."

Dale Ellis, a deadly outside shooter, gave this tip for young players: when shooting the ball, remember the four letters that spell out the word BEEF. The B, he said, stood for balance, which players must have to get off a good shot. The first E was for elbow, reminding him to keep his elbow parallel to the ground so that his forearm and his upper arm formed another letter shape, an L. The second E stressed keeping one's eyes on the target. Finally, the F meant to follow through after the ball left the fingertips.

Even though each decade has its share of superstars, in the 1980s a group of nearly 200 writers and broadcasters decided to honor the best of that ten-year span. In the Eastern Division the elite were: Michael Jordan and Isiah Thomas at the guard spots; Moses Malone as the center; and Larry Bird and Julius Erving as the forwards.

For the Western Division, the starting pivot man was Kareem Abdul-Jabbar, with his support on the front line being James Worthy and Alex English. The guards were George Gervin and Magic Johnson.

Amazingly, many players who are good enough to make it to the pro level set some records that are humbling. Wilt Chamberlain set a record by missing 5,805 free throws over his career, failing on 49% of his shots.

Opponents who couldn't stop the giant began to nullify some of his effectiveness by merely fouling him when it appeared he had an easy basket. If he was ready to dunk the ball, why not just hack him and send him to the line? After all, his career field goal percentage (54%) was actually higher than his free-throw percentage of 51! Such futility makes it almost impossible to believe he shot .875 from the charity stripe the night he drained 100 points.

Teammates said that his normal free-throw woes might have been partly psychological, as he would win informal foul-shooting games against them in practice sessions.

Chris Dudley, who lasted for many years in the NBA, was worse than Wilt Chamberlain at shooting free throws. He averaged a measly 46% for his career, with a season high of only .563 in his rookie season. Things got worse from there, as he shot below 40% in three seasons.

There was an NBA player who fouled out so often, he accumulated splinters from sitting on the bench at a record clip. Walter Dukes, a two-time All-Star who played in the league 1956 to 1963, actually was disqualified from 22% of the games he played, worse than any man ever. Players who commit that many fouls are sometimes called "hatchet" men.

•

Kevin Duckworth won the Most Improved Player trophy for 1988. That season, the second-year player nearly tripled his scoring average from his first year while leading his Portland Trail Blazers to 53 victories.

Duckworth proved an old basketball adage to be true: you can't teach height. By his senior year in school, he had reached his adult height of 7'. Even then, major colleges ignored him, so it was off to Eastern-Illinois for his college career (13.3 ppg over four seasons there). In the NBA, the 33rd selection in the draft was traded by his first team, the San Antonio Spurs, to Portland a few months after drafting him.

Once Duckworth was given the starting nod for the Trail Blazers, he cranked out a 22+ ppg average with about nine rebounds each night. It helped, too, that he hit the weights and trimmed down from a blimp-like high of 360 pounds to a muscular 280. It was quite a turn-about story for a guy who had been cut from the team as a high school freshman.

Manute Bol's wife was ready to walk away from the games at an Atlantic City casino, but elected to linger just a bit. A moment later she won $456,000 from a slot machine. One day later, Bol was fined $3,500 for throwing a punch at Anthony Mason, leaving Bol to think, "The money came in, and now some of it is flowing away."

The Bol family donated a large chunk of the casino winnings to his native country's famine relief fund.

NBA Players and Their Second Careers

Karl Malone once told reporters, "Ever since I was a little boy, I wanted to have my own trucking company. Trucking's my total love. That's what I always wanted, more than basketball." So, in the spring of 1992 he made his dream come true by buying a 48,000-pound, custom-made 18-wheeler. Adorned by an elaborate Western mural on both sides, the truck also housed a VCR, fax machine, and a microwave oven.

After Malone won gold medals in the Olympics in 1992 and 1996, he finally put the truck into service, hiring himself as the driver.

Charles Barkley tried his hand at acting. During the summer of 1992 he appeared on a television soap opera, "Santa Barbara."

The smooth Mark Price performed in what he called a "contemporary Christian singing group" in his spare time.

Wayman Tisdale was grooming himself for a singing career even while his NBA days were still productive. In 2004, his CD aptly entitled "Hang Time" was touted by Borders bookstores. They praised Tisdale as a "former NBA star turned bassist [who] still jams with the best as a towering force in jazz, filling his latest recording with one slam dunk after another."

Sean Elliott's pet project was opening a pet shop, which he called Full Court Pets as a play on words (full court press). Elliott, by the way, was the first man ever to make a comeback to play again in the NBA after receiving a kidney transplant. He played 71 games over two seasons after undergoing a transplant in 1999.

Harvey Grant said that he wanted to become a private eye. While it would seem he would be easy to spot (he stood 6' 9") if he was trying to trail a suspect, he insisted he'd be skilled at using his law enforcement degree from his college days.

Left-Handed Ballplayers

In 1990, a basketball publication listed an All-Lefty squad for players who were active then and a star-studded team of all-time greats who were left-handed. Starting with the unit from the 1990 era, the starting five consisted of Chris Mullin and Wayman Tisdale at the forward spots, David Robinson down low as the center, and guards Johnny Dawkins and John Lucas.

The bench was made up of three forwards—Sam Perkins, Stacey King, and Michael Cage; three men in the pivot—James Donaldson, Mark Eaton, and Brad Lohaus; and one guard, Sarunas Marciulionis.

The publication also listed the greatest lefties ever through 1990. Billy Cunningham and Dave Cowens, who actually played center (but did so at just 6' 9"), were the forwards. Since Cowens had a nice outside shot, playing forward was a logical move. The starting center was none other than Bill Russell, who won five MVP trophies over an eight-year span and who led the Celtics to eight straight championships and 11 over a 13-year period. Two outstanding playmakers handled the guard duties: Lenny Wilkens and Nate Archibald.

As would be expected, the bench on this team is packed with talent, too. Gail Goodrich (18.6 ppg lifetime), Dick Barnett, and Guy Rodgers were all excellent southpaw guards. Three big men round out the team: Willis Reed who won the MVP trophy for the regular season, the All-Star game, and the playoffs all in the same year, 1970; Artis Gilmore, who pumped in 22.3 ppg over his ABA career and led the NBA in field goal percentage four consecutive seasons; and, finally, Bob Lanier who averaged just over 20 ppg and more than 10 rpg for his entire NBA career.

●

A few years after the All-Lefty teams were selected, left-hander Derrick Coleman, who had awed everyone with his play at Syracuse, entered the league. Larry Nance pointed out why lefties can be so difficult to guard. "No matter how many times you go over it in the scouting reports, a left-handed big man has a huge advantage on guys who are used to guarding primarily right-handed guys who go to their right [when handling the ball]. Sometimes in the heat of the game, you don't even know who you're guarding. Or you do and you just forget that he's left-handed."

John "Hot Rod" Williams chuckled when he told of his first encounter with Coleman. "I had been out injured most of the season and I didn't know much about him. Then I go into the game, and I'm thinking he's going to go to his right like everyone else. Then all of the sudden boom! He goes left and dunks on me. Boy, was I surprised. I ran down the court and turned to Larry [Nance] and said, 'He is left-handed, I hope.'"

●

At the University of Maryland during the mid-1970s, the team employed a three-guard offense rather than the normal two. What made this even odder was the fact that two of the players were left-handed. John Lucas, a southpaw who excelled in tennis, was the star, but he was supported by Mo Howard and Brad Davis. Also noteworthy is the fact that all three played in the NBA.

▬ ▬ ▬

Pete Newell, once the Lakers general manager, considered himself, foremost, to be a teacher. He established the highly respected "Big Man Camp" which quickly gained fame among NBA players who were, well, big men. Newell worked with them on the intricacies of playing down in the low post.

Originally, he worked one-on-one with Kermit Washington, but when the word of Newell's teachings spread, he found himself training tons of stars. Newell believed that basketball was being "over-coached but under-taught," and he excelled as a mentor, drilling his big men to near perfection.

Newell limited his class size to a dozen and worked with men such as James Worthy. By 1990–1991, there were a whopping 82 players on NBA rosters who had been to Newell's camp.

Do players really appreciate the cheers of the home fans or do they block it out as they focus on the game at hand? When Artis Gilmore looked back on his days with the Chicago Bulls, a playoff-caliber team, he said, "The fans were a motivating factor, and we all felt the enthusiasm."

During one heated game versus Portland, Gilmore felt that the crowd's cheers actually "increased the tempo of both teams by 25 percent or maybe more. We were anxious to go out and perform, give them what they had paid to see."

In an oddity of the NBA, there was once a player whose last name had the same sound as the department that he led the league in. His name was Larry Steele and he did indeed lead all players in steals per game in 1973–1974 when he averaged 2.68 for the Portland Trail Blazers.

One writer joked that such an occurrence was unlikely ever to happen again. After all, he pointed out, "How many people have last names like Blocked Shots, Rebounds, or Scoring?"

Jack Kiser of the *Philadelphia Daily News* once interviewed Wilt Chamberlain, asking him to come up with a list of his all-time, All-Star team. The legendary center said, "Start off by putting Wilt Chamberlain at center. You want this to be an honest evaluation, don't you?

"You put Jerry West and Oscar Robertson at guards, because they are way ahead of anybody else. At forwards you have to go with Elgin Baylor and Bob Pettit and Rick Barry. The fourth forward would be Billy Cunningham, I guess because nobody hustled harder than him." He left Elvin Hayes off his list as he felt Hayes put up too many bad shots.

As for the guards who would come off his bench, Chamberlain went with Bob Cousy for his showmanship and John Havlicek along with Walt Frazier. He praised Havlicek's attitude, saying he was the kind of player who could only be stopped by shooting him in both legs.

He concluded by listing a backup center, Nate Thurmond. While many experts choose Bill Russell from the Chamberlain era as the second best center,

Chamberlain commented, "Nate was tougher on defense against me and was a much better scorer." He also explained that he felt "the Celtics just might have won as many titles if Nate had been their center. Russ would loaf on offense at least half the game. Nate never loafed a minute."

Not too long after Bill Walton's Portland Trail Blazers had won the NBA championship, he was asked to select four ideal teammates to round out a dream team (along with himself, of course). He rattled off five names, hedging a bit, "At one forward I'd take Maurice Lucas. The other forward would be Walter Davis, if he played better defense, but Bobby Gross is good, too. My two favorite guards are Lionel Hollins and Dennis Johnson." Gross's selection may have stunned some, but Gross worked at all the facets of the game and had been on the 1976–1977 Portland championship team with Walton (as did Hollins and Lucas).

Chuck Connors was perhaps the first man to destroy the backboard. In 1946, he dunked a ball so hard during warm-ups the glass backboard shattered. Back then the best they could come up with as a substitute was an old wooden backboard.

Between the years of 1959 and 1980 there were 21 NBA MVP Awards presented. On 20 of those occasions, the recipient of those honors was a center. The only exception was the utterly fantastic guard Oscar Robertson (in 1964), and it took a season in which he averaged a triple-double all year long for him to win the trophy!

SOURCES OF INFORMATION

The following sources were used for the quotes and information in this book:

BOOKS

Basketball's Hall of Fame, by Sandy Padwe

The Best Book of Basketball Facts and Stats, by Marty Strasen

Complete Handbook of Pro Basketball (1991 and 1992 editions). Editor: Zander Hollander

Giants: The 25 Greatest Centers of All Time, by Mark Heisler

NBA's Greatest, by John Hareas

Official NBA Encyclopedia (3rd edition)

On Court with the Superstars of the NBA, by Merv Harris

Tall Tales, by Terry Pluto

Who's Better, Who's Best in Basketball, by Elliott Kalb

PERIODICALS

Basketball Digest

Beckett Publications

Lindy's Pro Basketball 2004–05

Street and Smith Basketball Yearbooks

NEWSPAPERS

Elyria Chronicle Telegram

Morning Journal

Pittsburgh Post Gazette

Plain Dealer

WEB SITES

brainyquotes.com

greatquotes.com

nba.com

odaconline.com

u.arizona.edu

Index

About the Author

Wayne Stewart was born and raised in Donora, Pennsylvania, a town that has produced several big league baseball players, including Stan Musial and the father-son Griffeys. He now lives in Lorain, Ohio, and is married to Nancy (Panich) Stewart. They have two sons, Sean and Scott.

Wayne has covered the sports world as a writer for over 25 years now, beginning in 1978. He has interviewed and profiled many basketballs stars, including Kareem Abdul-Jabbar, Larry Bird, and Austin Carr, and baseball's legends such as Nolan Ryan, Bob Gibson, Tony Gwynn, Greg Maddux, Rickey Henderson, and Ken Griffey, Jr. He has written 17 baseball books to date, including *Baseball Oddities, Baseball Bafflers, Baseball Puzzlers, Indians on the Game, Fathers, Sons, and Baseball,* and juvenile baseball books featuring the history of big league franchises. Some of his works have also appeared in baseball anthologies.

Wayne has also written nearly 700 articles for national magazines such as *Baseball Digest, USA Today/Baseball Weekly, Boys' Life,* and also for Beckett Publications. He has also written for many major league official team publications, for teams such as the Braves, Yankees, White Sox, Orioles, Padres, Twins, Phillies, Red Sox, A's, and Dodgers. He has appeared, as a baseball expert/historian, on Cleveland's Fox 8 and on an ESPN Classic television show on Bob Feller. He also hosted his own radio shows at a small station in Lorain. These radio shows included a call-in, sports talk show; a pre-game Cleveland Indians report; Notre Dame pre-game shows; and broadcasts of local baseball contests.